Published Books

BERTOLT BRECHT

THE THREEPENNY OPERA

With the author's notes and
a foreword by Lotte Lenya

English book by
DESMOND VESEY

English lyrics by
ERIC BENTLEY

GROVE WEIDENFELD
NEW YORK

Published by Grove Weidenfeld
A division of Wheatland Corporation
841 Broadway
New York, NY 10003-4793

"August 28, 1928," by Lotte Lenya, originally published in *Theatre Arts*, May 1956, as "That Was a Time!," is reprinted by permission of the author.

Library of Congress Catalog Card Number: 64-8478
ISBN 0-8021-5039-X (pbk.)

Manufactured in the United States of America

Printed on acid-free paper

First Black Cat Edition 1964

30   29   28   27   26

It was Elisabeth Hauptmann, Bert Brecht's secretary and vigilant shadow in the mid-twenties, who first read of the great success in London of a revival of John Gay's *The Beggar's Opera*. She promptly ordered a copy of the play and, as soon as it arrived, began a rough translation whenever she had a few free moments, giving the German text to Brecht one scene at a time. Brecht was busily engaged on a play of his own, a most ambitious one which was promised to a producer; but at this early stage in his career he habitually kept *x* number of works-in-progress whirling around him (never throwing away so much as a scrap of paper on which he had scribbled two words). These bawds, bully boys and beggars of eighteenth-century London were creatures to delight his heart: why not make them speak his language in the fullest sense of the word? At odd intervals — for fun, for relaxation — he began fiddling with this scene or that, keeping intact what suited him, boldly adding or subtracting as he saw fit.

This always has been Brecht's procedure. As his admirers have it: to adapt, reinterpret, re-create, magnificently add modern social significance; or in his detractors' eyes: to pirate, plagiarize, shamelessly appropriate — to borrow at will from the vanished great like Marlowe and Shakespeare and Villon, and even from his actual or near contemporaries like Kipling and Gorky and Klabund. Critical storms have crashed around Brecht's close-cropped head for more than thirty years — some say the inevitable result of a singular talent, while others snort that they have been shrewdly provoked by a charlatan. "Why deny that Brecht steals?" said a Berlin friend last summer. "But — he steals with genius." Brecht generally has disdained self-defense and held to an enigmatic, smilingly scornful silence. Once another acquaintance rushed from table to table at the Café Romanische, claiming that he had found the real answer to Brecht's enigma on his bedside table — the dust-jacket of *Das Kapital* enclosing an Edgar Wallace thriller. But somebody pointed out that Brecht, who loves pranks and enigmas within enigmas, may well have planted it there to snare the snooper.

Whatever the exotic mixture of grist required to turn Brecht's creative mill, nobody doubts today that Elisabeth showed uncanny flair in turning up that copy of *The Beggar's Opera* during that winter of 1927-28. Almost at once Brecht called in Kurt Weill and announced that he had found a play for which Kurt might write "incidental music." Obviously the original Pepusch score no longer would do. Something as racy and biting, powerful and modern as Brecht's own language was called for, with as wide and daring a range of reference. No rush, of course, no deadline; time enough for that if a producer gave them the go-ahead after Brecht had shown around a few completed scenes.

This would be the second collaboration of Brecht and Weill, and their first complete play with music. It was Kurt who first had gone to see Brecht early in 1927 (as I remember). He had read poems by Brecht that had stirred him deeply, and which said in words what he felt increasingly drawn to say in music. He also knew Brecht had written one explosively controversial play, *Mann ist Mann,* produced in Darmstadt, that sounded close to his own ideas of theatre. Kurt had written three operas which had been applauded by the most austere music critics. Weill, Křenek, Hindemith were rated as the three most gifted young opera composers in Germany. But Kurt felt strongly that serious composers had withdrawn into too rarefied an atmosphere. He insisted that the widening gap between them and the great public must be bridged at all costs. "What do you want to become, a Verdi of the poor?" scoffingly asked his teacher Busoni. "Is that so bad?" Kurt had replied, deceptively mild. Now, at his first meeting with Brecht, Kurt discovered that Brecht seemed genuinely excited by the idea of writing something that required music. He himself played the guitar, sang old ballads amateurishly but with an odd magnetism, had even composed sketchy accompaniments to ballads that he had written. At the moment he had nothing for Kurt, but he promised to rummage in his head. Maybe there was an idea among the scraps of paper he had brought up in a willow basket from Augsburg, his Bavarian birthplace.

And suddenly he did turn up something, not a full play but a cycle of songs about an imaginary city on Florida's Gold Coast, called Mahagonny, to be sung by a mixture of real singers and straight actors, and tied together by a dramatic narrative. The setting was to be a boxing ring, but there were to be no backdrops: instead Caspar Neher would do a series of fantastic drawings to be flashed on a big screen. This is what has been named *Das Kleine Mahagonny,* and no modern work outside of Stravinsky's *Le Sacre du Printemps* ever created such a scandal at its première, which occurred at the snooty Baden-Baden Festival. Half the public cheered madly, the other half booed and whistled — and Brecht had provided his cast with toy whistles so that they could whistle back. By the way, I sang the prostitute Jenny at the insistence of both authors. Until then I had been a dancer and a straight actress, and never had studied singing. I couldn't read a note — exactly why I was chosen! Also, I sang my first song in English, taught me phonetically by Greta Keller: "Oh, moon of Alabama . . ."

But the hard-boiled Berlin theatre world had not been

impressed by our clamorous reception at a high-brow festival. If Brecht showed a few producers anything of *Bettler Oper,* as he now called it, no warmly receptive word came back to us. Kurt and I were living in the pension Hassforth on the Louisenplatz. Our two rooms were dominated by paintings of a hideously bloody deer hunt, and the furniture was painted pitch-black. (We called it "Grieneisen," after a famous Berlin funeral parlor.) Kurt had two or three pupils and painfully added a little extra to our meager income by writing criticism of radio musical programs. I got an occasional acting job, mostly in suburban theatres. But Kurt was always at his desk by nine (he rarely used the piano when working — except, as Ogden Nash was to note later, as a rest for his pipe), completely absorbed and like a happy child. This was never to change, as a daily routine, except for interruption for rehearsals or out-of-town tryouts. Brecht came very occasionally to Hassforth's: he preferred that people come to him, which suited Kurt perfectly, although when it was a matter of actual composing, he worked at home alone.

Brecht lived at that time in an attic studio with a skylight, near the intersection Am Knie: no rugs and no curtains to speak of, big iron stove to battle the drafts, typewriter on a massive table, easel on which stood drawings of costumes and sets, huge couch against the wall. On this couch and around the room lounged the ever-present disciples, male and female: the men with hair cropped, and wearing turtle-neck sweaters and slacks; the women without make-up, their hair skinned back, and wearing sweaters and skirts — this highly stylized proletarian style set by the master. Brecht alone stood, looking frail in those days, striding back and forth in a fetid blue cloud from his stogy, pausing for a quick question to this sitter, a snap reaction to a line from another, deep-set brown eyes forever blinking, small white hands continuously gesturing, translating everything into terms of theatre. Sometimes soundless laughter would shake him and he would slap his leg in an endearing way until the laughter ended in exhausting pants, leaving him to rub his eyes with the back of his hand and repeat, *"Ja, das Leben . . ."*

When Kurt arrived for a serious work session, the disciples would depart — most often Elisabeth and I stayed on — and the two men would start their discussion. Never have I known such a concentration of pure listening as Kurt could summon up, his face like a young seminarist's behind the thick glasses. His precise answers were made in a quiet, deep voice that held a slight hint of mockery — from shyness, not arrogance, as some people mistakenly thought. Brecht and Kurt had the most enormous respect for each other's opinions, though the relationship never deepened into a strong friendship (as it did between Kurt and Georg Kaiser, and later between Kurt and Maxwell Anderson). Sometimes Brecht impressed on Kurt his own ideas for a song, picking out chords on his guitar. Kurt noted these ideas with his grave little smile and invariably said yes, he would try to work them in when he got back to Hassforth's.

Early in 1928 we had not heard that a young German actor named Ernst-Josef Aufricht, deciding that he wanted to become a producer, had rented the Schiffbauerdamm Theater. It was — miraculously, still is — a wonderful old house, all red and white and gold, with plaster nymphs, Tritons and cherubs, adorably *kitsch*. Located in the principal theatre district, only a few steps from the bustling Friedrichstrasse, it had somehow been bypassed, obscured by big buildings on all sides, vaguely jinxed by repute. Aufricht optimistically began the search for a new play that would reopen his theatre in a blaze of glory. He engaged Heinrich Fischer as *dramaturg*, Erich Engel as director, and Caspar Neher as stage designer, then hounded publishers, pursued agents, haunted those legendary cafés where the gilded Bohemia met. Indeed, it was at Schlichter's that Aufricht remembers catching up with Bert Brecht. Yes, Brecht was deep in a play, but there was still much to be done. Besides, it was promised to another producer. Sorry — oh, he had another one, six scenes finished, written with his left hand. Well, yes, Aufricht could take a look at it. A few days later, on a drizzly afternoon, Aufricht's maid went to Brecht's studio for the manuscript and returned with its pages soaked through. Aufricht read it through, *dramaturg* Fischer read it through —and amazingly they found themselves wanting it! And for early fall production! No mention, it would appear, of music. Aufricht told me last summer that it wasn't until later, when Brecht brought in additional scenes, that he let it drop that there was to be incidental music by a certain Kurt Weill. Aufricht was horrified. Wasn't Weill that little boy with a reputation as an *enfant terrible* of atonal music? Well, that would be all right, he told Brecht. Secretly he engaged a young musician named Theo Mackeben to look up the original Pepusch music, which later could be substituted for the Weill score.

Then Aufricht advanced his date for the opening of the Schiffbauerdamm to August 28 — and all deadlines were terrifying to Brecht. A hurried consultation was held, and it was decided that the only way Brecht and Kurt could whip the work still ahead of them was to escape from Berlin. But to where? Somebody suggested a certain quiet little French Riviera resort. Wires went off for reservations, and on the first of June, Kurt and I left by train, while Brecht drove down with Helene Weigel and their son Stefan. The Brechts had rented a house near the *plage*. We had a room in a pension hotel not far away. The two men wrote and rewrote furiously, night and day, with only hurried swims in between. I recall Brecht wading out, pants rolled up, cap on head, stogy in mouth. I had been given the part of Spelunken-Jenny (Aufricht now says it was after my audition in the tango-ballad that he decided to forget about Pepusch), and Weigel was to play the brothel madam, so we studied our roles. When we got back to Berlin, Brecht and Kurt had ready a nearly complete script for Engel, the director. Neher's sets had been planned, and his drawings finished weeks before. The first rehearsal was upon us.

At no time in theatre history did a play draw near its opening in such an atmosphere of utter doom. The word around Berlin was that Aufricht, poor benighted amateur, was stuck with the turkey of all time. The disasters multiplied. Carola Neher, the ideal Polly, had rushed off to Davos to be with her dying husband Klabund. After frantic telephone calls, she was replaced by Roma Bahn. The actor who was to play Mr. Peachum — could it have been Peter Lorre? — backed out, and Erich Ponto was brought from Dresden. Harald Paulsen, our Mackie, from operetta, and Rosa Valletti, our Mrs. Peachum, a popular star in Berlin cabaret, shouted constant protests. Valletti — of all people, with her gamy repertory! — screamed that she wouldn't sing "those filthy words" in her "Ballad of Sexual Submissiveness" and on the last day of rehearsals signed a contract with another producer, confident that she would be free within the week. Helene Weigel suddenly burst out with a startling idea for her brothel madam — to play her legless à la Lon Chaney, pushing herself around on a wheeled platform — as suddenly, she was stricken with appendicitis and had to be replaced.

Paulsen, vain even for an actor, insisted that his entrance as Mackie Messer needed building up: why not a song right there, all about Mackie, getting in mention if possible of the sky-blue bow tie that he wanted to wear? Brecht made no comment but next morning came in with the verses for the "Moritat" of Mack the Knife and gave them to Kurt to set to music. This currently popular number, often called the most famous tune written in Europe during the past half century, was modeled after the *Moritaten* ("mord" meaning murder, "tat" meaning deed) sung by singers at street fairs, detailing the hideous crimes of notorious arch-fiends. Kurt not only produced the tune overnight, he knew the name of the hand-organ manufacturer — Zucco Maggio — who could supply the organ on which to grind out the tune for the prologue. And the "Moritat" went not to Paulsen but to Kurt Gerron, who doubled as Street Singer and Tiger Brown.

Among the distinguished kibitzers who wandered in and out of the stalls, I remember only one who contributed a truly brilliant suggestion — novelist and playwright Lion Feuchtwanger, who suggested a new title for the work: *Die Dreigroschenoper*. Brecht agreed and at once that name went up on the marquee. Actor Fritz Kortner joined with Aufricht and Engel in trying to persuade Kurt to remove the chorale at the close — "It's out of place, just like Bach." Neher told me years later that he had said to Kurt, "If you ever agree to that, I'll be finished with you forever." In any event the chorale stayed. What was supposed to be the final dress rehearsal, the night before the opening, lasted until after five in the morning. Everybody was completely distraught, shouting and swearing — everybody except Kurt Weill. The brothel scene was torn apart, begun over — and still didn't work. It was after five when I began singing my "Solomon Song" — which was interrupted by the cry, "Stop! Stop!" So that was cut; the show seemed to be running hours too long. We heard that Aufricht was asking people out front if they knew where he could find a new play in a hurry. Respected Berlin theatre oracles slipped out to spread the word that Brecht and Weill proposed to insult the public with a ludicrous mishmash of opera, operetta, cabaret, straight theatre, outlandish American jazz, not one thing or the other. Why didn't they withdraw the work before the opening?

Nor was there to be rest for any of us before the opening. By noon we were back in the theatre and started on a final run-through, only less hysterical because nobody was up to it. Moreover this had been an unusually warm summer, and the day was a hot one. It was late in the afternoon when suddenly a new voice was heard shouting in wild fury. It was Kurt, who had just discovered that my name inadvertently had been omitted from the program. For the first and the last time in his whole theatre career Kurt completely lost control — though not out of consideration for his own interest. Perhaps it was a blessing that I was the one who had to quiet him and assure him that, billing or no billing, nothing could keep me from going on.

There have been many accounts written of that opening night of *Dreigroschen*. It has so truly entered the realm of the fabulous that I shall be brief. Up to the stable scene the audience seemed cold and apathetic, as though convinced in advance that it had come to a certain flop. Then after the *Kanonen* song, an unbelievable roar went up, and from that point it was wonderfully, intoxicatingly clear that the public was with us. However, late the next morning as we were waiting for the first reviews, there persisted a crazy unreality about what had happened. Nobody quite dared believe in our success. Nor did the reviews confirm it for us — they were decidedly mixed. Hollander wrote that he had slept through the whole performance. Alfred Kerr, the most astute of them all, was greatly impressed, though he wondered if this was to be the new direction of the Berlin theatre. Kurt and I read hurriedly through Kerr's review to the last paragraph, which was headed: "WHO IS SHE?" "From what district does she come? With that lilt in her voice she must be Austrian . . ." He ended: "Watch her. Pretty soon she will be in the limelight." When we had finished with all the reviews, Kurt and I thought it should be possible to move from Hassforth's into a small flat of our own.

From that day Berlin was swept by a *Dreigroschenoper* fever. In the streets no other tunes were whistled. A *Dreigroschen* bar opened, where no other music was played. Immediately the "Brecht style" and the "Weill style" were slavishly imitated by other dramatists and composers. And Alfred Kerr's prophecy for me came true with dazzling speed. Walking through the Tiergarten I unthinkingly passed a blind beggar who called after me, "Fraülein Lenya, is it only on the stage that you notice a blind beggar?" Perhaps the strangest note of all is that people who scornfully had passed up that opening night began to lie about it, to claim to have been there, primed for a sure-fire sensation! Even now, anybody who passed through the Berlin of that period, and who comes backstage to see me at the Theatre de Lys in New York, twenty-eight years later, feels compelled to cry, "Of course I was there that opening night!" And though I remember that the Schiffbauerdamm had less than eight hundred seats, I nod. Why not, after all? Sometimes, remembering all that madness, even to that blank space in the program, I'm not even sure that I was there myself.

— LOTTE LENYA

THE THREEPENNY OPERA

CHARACTERS

MACHEATH, *nicknamed Mackie the Knife*

JONATHAN JEREMIAH PEACHUM,
   proprietor of the firm "The Beggar's Friend"

CELIA PEACHUM, *his wife*

POLLY PEACHUM, *his daughter*

BROWN, *chief of police in London*

LUCY, *his daughter*

GINNY JENNY

SMITH

THE REVEREND KIMBALL

FILCH

A ballad singer, the gang, beggars, whores, constables

PROLOGUE

Market Day in Soho

Beggars are begging, thieves thieving, whores whoring.
A ballad singer sings a Moritat.

THE MORITAT OF MACKIE THE KNIFE

And the shark he has his teeth and
There they are for all to see.
And Macheath he has his knife but
No one knows where it may be.

When the shark has had his dinner
There is blood upon his fins.
But Macheath he has his gloves on:
They say nothing of his sins.

All along the Thames Embankment
People fall down with a smack.
And it is not plague or cholera:
Word's around that Mac is back.

On a blue and balmy Sunday
Someone drops dead in the Strand.
And a man slips round the corner.
People say: Macheath's on hand.

And Schmul Meyer still is missing
Like many another rich young man.
And Macheath has got his money.
Try to prove *that* if you can!

PEACHUM *with his wife and daughter stroll across*
the stage from left to right.

3

Jenny Towler was discovered
With a jackknife in her breast.
And Macheath strolls down the dockside
Knows no more than all the rest.

Where is Alphonse Glite the coachman?
Was he stabbed or drowned or shot?
Maybe someone knows the answer.
As for Mackie, he does not.

One old man and seven children
Burnt to cinders in Soho.
In the crowd is Captain Mackie who
Is not asked and does not know.

And the widow not yet twenty
(Everybody calls her Miss)
Woke up and was violated.
What did Mackie pay for this?

There is a burst of laughter from the whores, and a man steps out from among them and walks quickly across the stage and exit.

GINNY JENNY: Look! That was Mackie the Knife!

ACT ONE

I

IN ORDER TO COMBAT THE INCREASING HARDHEARTEDNESS OF MEN, MR. J. PEACHUM, MAN OF BUSINESS, HAS OPENED A SHOP WHERE THE POOREST OF THE POOR MAY ACQUIRE AN APPEARANCE THAT WILL TOUCH THE STONIEST OF HEARTS

The Wardrobe Room of Jonathan Jeremiah Peachum's Establishment for Beggars

PEACHUM'S MORNING ANTHEM

Wake up, you old Image of Gawd!
Get on with your sinful backsliding!
Continue to perpetrate fraud!
Jehovah will do the providing!

Go barter your brother, you bear!
Sell your wife at an auction, you lout!
You think Our Lord God isn't there?
On Judgment Day you will find out.

PEACHUM *(to the audience):* Something new — that's what we *must* have. My business is too difficult. You see, my business is trying to arouse human pity. There are a few things that'll move people to pity, a few, but the trouble is, when they've been used several times, they no longer work. Human beings have the horrid capacity of being able to make themselves heartless at will. So it happens, for instance, that a man who sees another man on the street corner with only a stump for an arm will be so shocked the first time that he'll give him sixpence. But the second

5

time it'll be only a threepenny bit. And if he sees him a third time, he'll hand him over cold-bloodedly to the police. It's the same with these spiritual weapons.

A large board is let down from the flies and on it is written: "It is more blessed to give than to receive."

What's the use of the finest and most stirring sayings painted on the most enticing boards if they get used up so quickly? There are four or five sayings in the Bible that really touch the heart. But when they're used up, one's daily bread's just gone. Take that one there: "Give and it shall be given unto you" — how threadbare it has become in the three weeks we've had it. Always something new must be offered. We can fall back on the Bible again, but how often can *that* be done?

There is a knock. PEACHUM *opens the door, and a young man named* FILCH *enters.*

FILCH: Peachum & Co.?

PEACHUM: Peachum.

FILCH: Then you're the owner of the firm called "The Beggars' Friend"? I was sent to you. Oh, those sayings! What an investment! I suppose you've got a whole library of such things? Well, that's something quite different! Fellows like us — we'd never get an idea like that, and not being properly educated, how could business ever flourish?

PEACHUM: Your name?

FILCH: Well, you see, Mr. Peachum, I've had bad luck ever since I was a boy. My mother was a drunkard, my father a gambler. From an early age I had to fend for myself. And without the loving hand of a mother to guide me I sank deeper and deeper into the morass of the great city. I never knew a father's care or the blessings of a contented home. So now you see me . . .

PEACHUM: So now I see you . . .

FILCH (confused): . . . see me . . . completely destitute, a prey to my own desires.

PEACHUM: Like a wreck on the high seas, and so on. Tell me, wreck, in which district do you recite this nursery rhyme?

FILCH: What do you mean, Mr. Peachum?

PEACHUM: Of course, you deliver this speech in public?

FILCH: Yes, you see, Mr. Peachum, there was a nasty little incident yesterday in Highland Street. I was standing quietly and miserably at the corner, hat in hand, not meaning any harm. . . .

PEACHUM (turning over the pages of a notebook): Highland Street. Yes. That's the one. You're the crawling blackleg that Honey and Sam caught yesterday. You had the impertinence to solicit passers-by in District 10. We let it go at a good beating, as we took it you didn't know where God lives. But if you let yourself be seen there again, we shall have to use the saw. Understand?

FILCH: Please, Mr. Peachum, please! What can I do then, Mr. Peachum? The gentlemen really beat me black and blue, and then they gave me your business card. If I was to take off my coat, you'd think you was looking at a mackerel.

PEACHUM: My young friend, if you don't look like a flounder, my people were a sight too easy with you. This young sprout comes along and imagines that if he sticks out his paws he'll be all set for a juicy steak. What would you say if someone took the best trout out of your pond?

FILCH: But you see, Mr. Peachum — I haven't got a pond.

PEACHUM: Well, licenses are only granted to professionals. (*He points in a businesslike way to a large map of London.*) London is divided into fourteen districts. Everyone wishing to ply the begging-trade in any one of them has to have a license from Jonathan Jeremiah Peachum and Company. My God, anyone could come along — "a prey to his own desires"!

FILCH: Mr. Peachum. Only a few shillings stand between me and total ruin. I *must* be able to do something with two shillings in hand. . . .

PEACHUM: One pound.

FILCH: Mr. Peachum! (FILCH *points beseechingly at a poster which reads: "Shut not your ears to misery."*)

PEACHUM *points to a curtain in front of a showcase, on which is written: "Give and it shall be given unto you."*

FILCH: Ten shillings.

PEACHUM: And fifty per cent of the weekly takings. Including outfit, seventy per cent.

FILCH: And please, what does the outfit consist of?

PEACHUM: The firm decides that.

FILCH: Well, what district can I start on?

PEACHUM: Top half of Baker Street. That'll be a bit cheaper. It's only fifty per cent there, including outfit.

FILCH: Thank you. (*He pays.*)

PEACHUM: Your full name?

FILCH: Charles Filch.

PEACHUM: Correct. (*Shouts.*) Mrs. Peachum!

MRS. PEACHUM *enters.*

This is Filch. Number 314, Upper Baker Street. I'll enter it myself. Of course, you would want to start now, just before the Coronation — the chance of a lifetime to earn a little money. Outfit C for you. (*He

draws back the linen curtain in front of a showcase in
which are standing five wax models.)

FILCH: What's that?

PEACHUM: These are the five basic types of misery best
adapted to touching the human heart. The sight of
them induces that unnatural state of mind in which a
man is actually willing to give money away.

Outfit A: Victim of the Progress of Modern Traffic.
The Cheerful Cripple, always good-tempered — *(He
demonstrates it.)* — always carefree, effect heightened
by a mutilated arm.

Outfit B: Victim of the Art of War. The Troublesome
Twitcher, annoys passers-by, his job is to arouse
disgust — *(He demonstrates it.)* — modified by medals.

Outfit C: Victim of the Industrial Boom. The Pitiable
Blind, or the High School of the Art of Begging.
*(PEACHUM displays him, advancing unsteadily toward
FILCH. At the moment when he bumps into FILCH, the
latter screams with horror. PEACHUM stops instantly,
gazes at him in amazement, and suddenly roars:)* He
feels pity! You'll never make a beggar — not in a
lifetime. That sort of behavior is only fit for the
passers-by! Then it's Outfit D! — Celia, you've been
drinking again! And now you can't see out of your
eyes. Number 136 has been complaining about his
neck-rag. How often must I tell you a gentleman will
not have filthy clothing next to his skin. Number 136
has paid for a brand-new costume. The stains — the
only thing about it capable of awakening pity —
were to be put on by neatly ironing in paraffin wax!
Never trouble to think! Always have to do everything
oneself. *(To FILCH:)* Undress and put this on, but keep
it in good condition!

FILCH: And what happens to my things?

PEACHUM: Property of the firm. Outfit E: Young man who's seen better days, preferably one who "never thought he would come down to this."

FILCH: Oh, so you're using that too. Why can't *I* have the better days outfit?

PEACHUM: Because nobody believes in his own misery, my boy. If you've got the stomach-ache and say so, it only sounds disgusting. Anyway, it's not for you to ask questions. Just put these things on.

FILCH: Aren't they rather dirty?

PEACHUM *gives him a piercing glance.*

I'm sorry, Mr. Peachum, I'm sorry.

MRS. PEACHUM: Get a move on, sonny, I'm not going to hold your trousers till Christmas.

FILCH (*suddenly with great determination*): But I'm not going to take my shoes off! Not for anything. I'd rather chuck the whole thing. They were the only present I had from my poor mother, and never, never, however low I may have fallen . . .

MRS. PEACHUM: Don't talk rubbish. I know you've got dirty feet.

FILCH: Well, where do you expect me to wash my feet? In the middle of winter?

MRS. PEACHUM *leads him behind a folding screen, then sits down left and begins ironing candle-grease into a suit.*

PEACHUM: Where's your daughter?

MRS. PEACHUM: Polly? Upstairs.

PEACHUM: Was that man here again yesterday? The one who always comes when I'm out?

MRS. PEACHUM: Don't be so suspicious, Jonathan! There isn't a finer gentleman alive, and the Captain takes quite an interest in our Polly.

PEACHUM: Um.

MRS. PEACHUM: And if I can see an inch before my nose, Polly is fond of him too.

PEACHUM: There you go, Celia! Throwing your daughter around as if I were a millionaire! So she's going to marry! And do you think our miserable business would last another week if the filthy customers had only *our* legs to look at? A husband! He'd soon have us in his clutches. That he would. Do you think your daughter would be any better than you at keeping her mouth shut in bed?

MRS. PEACHUM: You've got a nice opinion of your daughter!

PEACHUM: The worst! The very worst! She is nothing but a mass of sensuality.

MRS. PEACHUM: Well, she certainly doesn't get that from you!

PEACHUM: Marry! My daughter should be to me what bread is to the starving. *(He thumbs through the Bible.)* That's actually written somewhere in the Bible. Marriage is a disgusting business anyhow. I'll soon beat the marriage out of her.

MRS. PEACHUM: Jonathan, you're just ignorant.

PEACHUM: Ignorant! What's his name, then — this *gentleman*?

MRS. PEACHUM: People just call him always "The Captain."

PEACHUM: So you haven't even asked him his name! Very nice!

MRS. PEACHUM: Well, we wouldn't be so ill-bred as to ask him for his birth certificate; him being such a gentleman, inviting us to the Octopus Hotel for a little hop.

PEACHUM: Where!

MRS. PEACHUM: To the Octopus. For a little hop.

PEACHUM: Captain? Octopus Hotel? I see —

MRS. PEACHUM: The gentleman never touched me and my daughter except with kid gloves on.

PEACHUM: Kid gloves!

MRS. PEACHUM: Now I come to think of it, he always has gloves on — white ones, white kid gloves.

PEACHUM: Ah! White kid gloves and a stick with an ivory handle and spats over his patent leather shoes and a nice polite manner and a scar . . .

MRS. PEACHUM: On his neck. How do you know all this about him?

FILCH *comes out.*

FILCH: Mr. Peachum, could you give me a few tips on what to do? I always like to have a system and not go at things haphazard.

MRS. PEACHUM: He wants a system!

PEACHUM: He can be an idiot. Come back this evening at six and you'll be given the necessaries. Now, get out!

FILCH: Thank you, Mr. Peachum, thank you very much. *(Exit.)*

PEACHUM: Fifty per cent! — And now I'll tell you who this gentleman with the kid gloves is — he's Mackie the Knife!

He runs up the stairs into POLLY's *bedroom.*

MRS. PEACHUM: Lord save us! Mackie the Knife! Jesus, Mary and Joseph! Polly! Where's Polly!

PEACHUM *comes slowly downstairs.*

PEACHUM: Polly? Polly hasn't been home. Her bed's not touched.

MRS. PEACHUM: Then she's been having supper with that wool merchant. I'm certain of it, Jonathan.

PEACHUM: For our sake, I hope it was the wool merchant.

MR. *and* MRS. PEACHUM *step in front of the curtain and sing. Song illumination: a golden light. The organ is lit up. Three lights come down on a bar from above, and on a board is written:*

THE I-FOR-ONE SONG

PEACHUM:
I for one
Like to spend the night at home and in my bed.
She prefers fun:
Does she think the Lord keeps busy pouring manna on
    her head?

MRS. PEACHUM:
Such is the moon over Soho
Such is that magic "Can you feel my heart beating" spell
Oh, it's "Whither thou goest, I will go with thee, Johnny"
And the new moon's shining on the asphodel.

PEACHUM:
I for one
Like to do what has a purpose and a goal.
They prefer fun:
After which of course they end up in the hole.

BOTH:
So where is their moon over Soho?
What's left of their confounded "Can you feel my heart
    beating" spell?
Where now is their "Whither thou goest, I will go with
    thee, Johnny!"
For the old moon's waning and you're shot to hell!

2

DEEP IN THE HEART OF SOHO, MACKIE THE KNIFE CELE-
BRATES HIS WEDDING WITH POLLY PEACHUM, DAUGHTER
OF THE KING OF THE BEGGARS

An Empty Stable

MATTHEW (*nicknamed "Money Matthew," carrying a lantern and pointing a revolver round the stable*): Hi! Hands up, if anyone's there!

MACHEATH *enters and walks round by the front of the stage.*

MACHEATH: Well? Is anyone here?

MATTHEW: Not a soul. We can have our marriage here safe enough.

POLLY (*enters in a wedding dress*): But this is a stable!

MACHEATH: Sit down on the crib for a while, Polly. (*To the audience:*) Today, in this stable, my marriage to Miss Polly Peachum will be celebrated; she has followed me for love, in order to share the rest of my life with me.

MATTHEW: A lot of people in London will be saying this is the riskiest thing you've ever done, luring Mr. Peachum's only child out of his own house.

MACHEATH: Who *is* Mr. Peachum?

MATTHEW: He himself would say he was the poorest man in London.

POLLY: But you're not thinking of having our marriage here? It's just a nasty, common stable. You can't invite the clergyman here. And besides, it isn't even ours. We really ought not to begin our new life with a burglary, Mac. This is the happiest day of our lives!

MACHEATH: Dearest child, everything shall be as you wish. Not a stone shall touch your little feet. The furnishings are on the way at this very moment.

MATTHEW: Here comes the furniture!

There is a sound of heavy wagons arriving. Half a dozen men enter, carrying furniture, carpets, crockery, etc., and soon the stable is transformed into an over-ornate living room.[1]

MACHEATH: Junk!

The men place their presents down on the left, congratulate the bride, and report to the bridegroom.[2]

JACOB *(nicknamed "Hook-finger Jacob")*: Here's luck! At 14 Ginger Street there were some people on the second floor. We had to smoke 'em out.

ROBERT *(nicknamed "Robert the Saw")*: Good luck! A copper in the Strand got in our way.

MACHEATH: Amateurs!

ED: We did what we could, but three people in the West End are goners. Good luck!

MACHEATH: Amateurs and bunglers!

JIMMY: An old gentleman got something he wasn't expecting. I don't think it's serious. Luck!

MACHEATH: My orders were: bloodshed to be avoided. It makes me quite sick when I think of it. *You'll* never make businessmen. Cannibals — but never businessmen!

WALTER: *(nicknamed "Wally the Weeper")*: Good luck! Half an hour ago, madam, that harpsichord still belonged to the Dutchess of Somerset!

POLLY: Whatever furniture is this?

MACHEATH: How do you like it, Polly?

---

* Numerals in the text refer to the "Tips for Actors" on p. 103.

POLLY *(crying)*: All those poor people, just for a few bits of furniture!

MACHEATH: And what furniture! Junk! You're right to be angry. A rosewood harpsichord — and a Renaissance sofa That's unforgivable. And where's a table?

WALTER: A table?

They lay planks across the feeding troughs.

POLLY: Oh, Mac, I'm so unhappy. Let's hope anyhow the clergyman won't come!

MATTHEW: But he will. *We* told him the way quite clearly.

WALTER *(pushes forward the improvised table)*: A table!

MACHEATH *(seeing POLLY crying)*: My wife is upset. And where are the other chairs? A harpsichord and no chairs! Never trouble to think. How often does it happen that I have a wedding? Shut your trap, Weeper! How often does it happen, I'm asking, that I leave anything to you? It makes my wife unhappy from the start.

ED: Dear Polly . . .

MACHEATH *(knocking his hat from his head[3])*: "Dear Polly!" I'll knock your head into your guts with your "dear Polly," you sewer rat! Whoever heard the like — "dear Polly"! Maybe you've slept with her?

POLLY: But Mac . . .

ED: I swear that . . . !

WALTER: Madam, if there's anything more you'd like here, we'll go out again . . .

MACHEATH: A rosewood harpsichord and no chairs! *(Laughs.)* What do you say to that, as the bride?

POLLY: Well, it could be worse.

MACHEATH: Two chairs and a sofa, and the bridal pair sit on the ground.

POLLY: Yes, that's a fine thing.

MACHEATH *(sharply)*: Saw the legs off the harpsichord! Come on! Come on!

Four of the men saw the legs off the harpsichord and sing:

> Bill Lawgen and Mary Syer
> They were spliced last Tuesday night by law!
> Where the bride's gown came from he did not know
> She'd no name for her man but So and So
> And yet they got a license from the Registrar!
> (A toast!)

WALTER: And so, all's well that ends well. We have another bench, madam.

MACHEATH: Might I now request you gentlemen to take off your rags and dress yourselves respectably? After all, this isn't the wedding of a nobody. And Polly, may I ask you to get busy with the grub hampers?

POLLY: Is that the wedding breakfast? Is it all stolen, Mac?

MACHEATH: Of course, of course.

POLLY: I'd like to know what you'd do if there was a knock on the door and the sheriff came in!

MACHEATH: Then I'd show you what your husband *can* do.

MATTHEW: Not a chance of it today. All the police are lining the streets. The Queen's coming to town for the Coronation on Friday.

POLLY: Two knives and fourteen forks! A knife for each chair!

MACHEATH: What a wash out! That's the work of apprentices, not trained men. Haven't you any idea of style? You ought to be able to tell the difference between Chippendale and Louis Quatorze.

The rest of the gang now return, wearing smart evening dress, but their behavior during the rest of the scene is unfortunately not in keeping with their attire.

WALTER: We wanted to bring the most valuable things. Look at that wood! The material is absolutely first-class.

MATTHEW: Sssst! Permit me, Captain . . .

MACHEATH: Come here, Polly.

The two of them pose for congratulations.

MATTHEW: Permit me, Captain, on behalf of all, on the happiest day of your life, the springtide of your career — its turning point, one might say — to offer you our heartiest congratulations and . . . so forth. It's horrible — this gassy talk. Well, anyway — (*Shakes* MACHEATH's *hand.*) — chin up, boys!

MACHEATH: Thank you. That was very nice of you, Matthew.

MATTHEW (*shaking* POLLY's *hand, after having patted* MACHEATH *affectionately on the back*): Ah, it's spoken from the heart! Well, keep your head up, old man, I mean — (*Grinning.*) — as far as your head's concerned never let it droop.

Roars of laughter from the men. MACHEATH *suddenly catches hold of* MATTHEW *and gently jerks him to the floor.*

MACHEATH: Hold your trap. Keep your dirty jokes for your Kitty: she's the right slut for them.

POLLY: Mac, don't be so common.

MATTHEW: I object to you calling Kitty a slut . . . (*Stands up with difficulty.*)

MACHEATH: Oh! You object, do you?

MATTHEW: And what's more, I never have dirty jokes for her. I respect Kitty far too much for that. Which maybe you can't understand, being made the way you are. And you ought to know about dirty jokes! You think Lucy hasn't told me the things you've said to her? I'm a kid-gloves gent compared to that.

MACHEATH *gives him a look.*

JACOB: Stop it. This is a wedding! *(They pull him back.)*

MACHEATH: A fine wedding, eh, Polly? To see these gutter-rats all round you on the day of your marriage? You never thought your husband would be let down by his friends like this. That'll teach you.

POLLY: I think it's nice.

ROBERT: Tripe! No one's letting you down. A little difference of opinion can happen any time. Your Kitty is as good as anyone else. Now come on with the wedding present, my boy.

ALL: Come on, get on with it!

MATTHEW *(offended)*: There!

POLLY: Oh! A wedding present! How sweet of you, Mr. Money Matthew! Look, Mac, what a lovely nightdress!

MATTHEW: Another dirty joke, eh, Captain?

MACHEATH: All right, now. Didn't want to offend you on this festive occasion.

WALTER: Well, and what about this? Chippendale! *(He uncovers an immense Chippendale grandfather clock.)*

MACHEATH: Quatorze.

POLLY: It's wonderful. I'm so happy. I can't find words, your kindness is so fantastic. A shame we haven't a home for it, isn't it Mac?

MACHEATH: Think of it as a beginning. All beginnings are difficult. Many thanks, Walter. Now clear the stuff away — food.

JACOB *(while the others are laying the table)*: Of course, I've forgotten to bring anything. *(Emphatically to*

POLLY:) Believe me, young lady, I feel very embarrassed.

POLLY: Don't mention it, Mr. Hook-Finger Jacob.

JACOB: All the boys throw their presents around and I stand here with nothing. Put yourself in my place. But this always happens to me! I could tell you of some fixes I've been in! Boy! You wouldn't believe them! The other day I met Ginny Jenny and said to her, "Now look, you old cow," I said . . .

He suddenly sees MACHEATH *standing behind him and walks away without a word.*

MACHEATH (*leads* POLLY *to her seat*): This is the finest food you'll get anywhere today, Polly. Shall we start?

They all sit down to the wedding breakfast.[4]

ED (*pointing to the service*): Lovely plates, Savoy Hotel.

JACOB: The egg mayonnaise is from Selfridge's. We had a jar of goose liver too. But on the way here Jimmy ate it out of spite. He said he had an empty belly.

WALTER: Respectable people don't say "belly."

JIMMY: And, Ed, don't gobble your eggs so, today of all days!

MACHEATH: Can't someone sing something? Something delightful?

MATTHEW (*choking with laughter*): Something delightful! That's a proper word! (*Under* MACBETH's *annihilating glance, he sits down, embarrassed.*)

MACHEATH (*knocking a dish out of someone's hand*): As a matter of fact, I didn't wish to start eating yet. Instead of this "On-with-the-food-and-into-the-trough" exhibition from you men, I'd have preferred something festive. Other people always do some such thing on a day like this.

JACOB: What sort of thing?

MACHEATH: Must I think of everything myself? I'm not asking for an opera here. But you might have arranged something more than eating and telling dirty jokes — well, a day like this just shows how far one can count on one's friends.

POLLY: The smoked salmon's wonderful, Mac.

ED: I'll bet you've never ate salmon like it. Mac has it every day. You're in the honeypot all right. I always said Mac'll make a fine match for a girl with a feeling for higher things. I said so to Lucy yesterday.

POLLY: Lucy? Who is Lucy, Mac?

JACOB (*embarrassed*): Lucy? Well, you know, you mustn't take it so seriously.

MATTHEW *has stood up and is making furious gestures behind* POLLY *to silence* JACOB.

POLLY (*sees him*): Are you wanting something? The salt? What were you going to say, Mr. Jacob?

JACOB: Oh nothing. Nothing at all. I really wasn't going to say anything. I'll be getting my tongue burnt.

MACHEATH: What have you got in your hand, Jacob?

JACOB: A knife, Captain.

MACHEATH: And what have you got on your plate?

JACOB: A trout, Captain.

MACHEATH: I see. And with the knife, I believe, you are eating the trout. That is unheard of, Jacob. Have you ever seen such a thing, Polly? Eating fish with a knife! A person who does that is a pig, do you understand me, Jacob? Try to learn! — You'll have a lot to do, Polly, before you can teach such oafs to behave like gentlemen. Do you even know what the word means: a gentleman?

WALTER: I know the difference from a woman!

POLLY: Oh, Mr. Walter!

MACHEATH: Well, don't you want to sing a song? Nothing to brighten up the day a bit? It's to be just another damn, sad, ordinary, dirty day like any other? And is anyone keeping watch at the door? Maybe you'd like me to do that? Perhaps I should stand guard at the door, today of all days, so you can stuff yourselves here at my expense?

WALTER (*sullenly*): What do you mean: at my expense?

JIMMY: Shut up, Wally. I'll go out. Who'd come here anyway? (*Exit.*)

JACOB: It'd be funny if all the wedding guests were copped today!

JIMMY (*bursts in*): Captain, the coppers!

WALTER: Tiger Brown!

MATTHEW: Garn, it's the Reverend Kimball.

KIMBALL *enters*.

ALL (*shout*): Good evening, Reverend Kimball!

KIMBALL: Well, well, well, so I've found you at last! In a little hut I find you; a small place, indeed, but your own.

MACHEATH: The Duke of Devonshire's.

POLLY: How do you do, your Reverence. I'm so happy you've come, on the happiest day of our lives . . .

MACHEATH: I request an anthem for the Reverend Kimball.

MATTHEW: How about "Bill Lawgen and Mary Syer"?

JACOB: That's right, "Bill Lawgen" should do.

KIMBALL: It would be pleasing to hear your voices raised in song, my men.

MATTHEW: Let's begin, gents.

Three of the men stand up and sing, hesitating, flat and uncertain.

WEDDING SONG FOR POORER PEOPLE

Bill Lawgen and Mary Syer
They were spliced last Tuesday night by law!
(I give you Bill and Mary, Gawd bless 'em!)
Where the bride's gown came from he did not know
She'd no name for her man but So and So
And yet they got a license from the Registrar!
(A toast!)

Do you know what your good wife does? No!
Will you let her go on doing it? No!
(I give you Bill and Mary, Gawd bless 'em!)
Billy Lawgen said to me: It's fine
So long as just one part of her is mine.
(The swine!)

MACHEATH: Is that all? Paltry!

MATTHEW (*choking again*): Paltry! Just the right word, gents. Paltry.

MACHEATH: Hold your trap!

MATTHEW: Well, I meant — no life, no swing, nothing!

POLLY: Gentlemen, if nobody will do anything, I myself will sing a little song as best I can, and in it I'm going to imitate a girl I once saw in a little bar in Soho. She was the washing-up skivvy, and I must tell you that everyone laughed at her, and then one day she spoke to the customers and told them the things I am going to sing to you now. So this is the little bar — you must imagine it being filthy dirty — and she stood behind it from morning to night. There's her slop pail and that's the cloth she used for drying the glasses. Where you are sitting, sat the men who laughed at her. You can laugh, too, so that everything is just as it was; but if you can't, then you needn't. (*She begins, pretending to wash glasses and muttering to herself.*) Now one

of you must say — you for instance, Mr. Walter —
(*Pointing at* WALTER:) — "And when is your ship
coming home, Jenny?"

WALTER: And when is your ship coming home, Jenny?

POLLY: And another says — you, perhaps: "Do you still
wash up the glasses, Pirate Jenny."

MATTHEW: Do you still wash up the glasses, Pirate Jenny?

POLLY: Yes, and now I'll begin.

*Song illumination: golden light. The organ is lit up.
Three lights on a bar come from above, and on a
board is written:*

PIRATE JENNY

Gentlemen, today you see me washing up the glasses
And making up the beds and cleaning.
When you give me p'raps a penny, I will curtsey rather
well.
When you see my tatty clothing and this tatty old hotel
P'raps you little guess with whom you're dealing.
One fine afternoon there will be shouting from the harbor.
Folk will ask. what's the reason for that shout?
They will see me smiling while I rinse the glasses
And will say: what has she to smile about?
        And a ship with eight sails and
        With fifty great cannon
        Sails in to the quay.

They say: go and wipe your glasses, my girl
And their pennies are thrown to me.
And I thank them for the pennies and I do the beds up
right
(Though nobody is going to sleep in them that night)
And they haven't the least idea who I may be.
One fine afternoon there will be roaring from the harbor.

Folk will ask: what's the reason for that roar?
They will see me standing just beside the window
And will say: now what's she sneering for?
    And the ship with eight sails and
    With fifty great cannon
    Will shoot up the town.

Gentlemen, I fear this puts an end to your laughter
For your walls, they will all cave in.
And this whole fair city will be razed to the ground.
Just one tatty old hotel will survive safe and sound.
Folk will ask what special person dwells therein.
And all night long round this hotel there will be shouting.
Folk will ask: why was it this they'd spare?
Folk will see me leave the place the following morning
And will say: so that's who was in there!
    And the ship with eight sails and
    With fifty great cannon
    Will run flags up the mast.

And a hundred men will come ashore before it's noon
And will go where it's dark and chill.
And every man they find, they will drag along the street
And they'll clap him in chains and lay him at my feet
And they'll ask: now which of these are we to kill?
And when the clock strikes noon it will be still down by
  the harbor.
When folk ask: now just who has got to die?
You will hear me say at that point: All of them!
And when their heads fall, I'll say: Whoopee!
    And the ship with eight sails and
    With fifty great cannon
    Will sail off with me.

MATTHEW: Very nice, comic, eh? How she does it, the
    young lady!

MACHEATH: What d'you mean: *nice*? That's art, not nice. You did it wonderfully, Polly. But before such swine — pardon me, your Reverence — there's no point, it's wasted. (*In an undertone to* POLLY:) Anyway, I don't approve of your doing this play-acting, kindly drop it in future.

Loud laughter at the table. The gang are making fun of the parson.

What have you got in your hand, your Reverence?

JACOB: Two knives, Captain.

MACHEATH: And what have you got on your plate, your Reverence?

KIMBALL: Smoked salmon, I think.

MACHEATH: And with the knife, I believe, you're eating the salmon?

JACOB: Have you ever seen the like, eating fish with a knife! A person who does that is nothing more than a . . .

MACHEATH: Pig. Understand me, Jacob? That'll teach you.

JIMMY (*bursting in*): Captain! The coppers! It's the sheriff himself.

WALTER: Brown! Tiger Brown!

MACHEATH: Yes, Tiger Brown it is. It's Tiger Brown, Sheriff of London and pillar of the Old Bailey, who is about to enter Captain Macheath's poor little abode. Now you'll learn something!

The gang creep away.

JACOB: It's the gallows for us.

BROWN *enters.*

MACHEATH: Hello, Jacky!

BROWN: Hello, Mac! Now I haven't got much time, I must

leave in a minute. Do you *have* to pick on somebody else's stable? *Another* burglary.

MACHEATH: But Jacky, it's so convenient. I'm delighted you could come to partake of old Mac's wedding breakfast. May I introduce my wife, Polly, née Peachum. Polly, this is Tiger Brown. Eh, old man? *(Slaps him on the back.)* And these are my friends, Jacky. You've probably seen them all before.

BROWN *(in embarrassment)*: I'm here in my private capacity, Mac.

MACHEATH: So are they. *(He calls them. They come, hands up.)* Hi, Jacob!

BROWN: That's Hook-Finger Jacob, he's a dirty skunk.

MACHEATH: Here! Jimmy! Robert! Walter!

BROWN: Well, we'll forget it for today.

MACHEATH: Hi, Ed! Matthew!

BROWN: Sit down, gentlemen, sit down.

ALL: Thank you, sir.

BROWN: Happy to meet the charming wife of my old friend Mac.

POLLY: Don't mention it, sir.

MACHEATH: Sit yourself down, you old rascal, and start in on the whisky! Polly! Gentlemen! Today you see in your midst a man whom our sovereign's inscrutable wisdom has chosen to set high over his fellow men, and who yet has remained through fair weather and foul my friend. You all know who I mean, and you, too, know who I mean, Brown. Ah, Jacky, do you remember when you were a soldier and I was a soldier and we served together in India? Jacky, old man, shall we sing them the "Song of the Heavy Cannon"? *(They sit side by side on the table.)*

Song illumination: a golden light. The organ is lit up. Three lights come down from above on a bar, and on a board is written:

The Song of the Heavy Cannon

John was a soldier and so was James
And George became a sergeant in short order.
But the army is not interested in names:
They were soon marching north to the border.
What soldiers live on
Is heavy cannon
From the Cape to Cutch Behar.
If it should rain one night
And they should chance to sight
Pallid or swarthy faces
Of uncongenial races
They'll maybe chop them up to make some beefsteak
 tartare.

Now John was rather cold at night
And James, he found the whisky "rather hot, sir."
But George said: "Everything's all right
For the army simply cannot go to pot, sir."
What soldiers live on
Is heavy cannon
From the Cape to Cutch Behar.
If it should rain one night
And they should chance to sight
Pallid or swarthy faces
Of uncongenial races
They'll maybe chop them up to make some beefsteak
 tartare.

John's gone west and James is dead
And George is missing and barmy.
Blood, however, is still blood-red:
They're recruiting again for the army.

 *As they all sit there, they march in time with their
 feet.*

What soldiers live on
Is heavy cannon
From the Cape to Cutch Behar.
If it should rain one night
And they should chance to sight
Pallid or swarthy faces
Of uncongenial races
They'll maybe chop them up to make some beefsteak
    tartare.

MACHEATH: We were boyhood friends, and though the
    great tides of life have swept us far apart, although
    our professional interests are quite different — some
    might even say diametrically opposed — our friend-
    ship has survived it all. That'll teach you something.
    Castor and Pollux, Hector and Andromache, and so
    forth. Seldom have I, the simple hold-up man — well,
    you know what I mean — seldom have I undertaken
    the smallest job without giving my friend Brown a
    share of the proceeds (a considerable share, Brown)
    as a token and a proof of my unswerving loyalty to
    him. And seldom has the all-powerful Sheriff — take
    that knife out of your mouth, Jacob — organized a
    raid without previously giving a little tip-off to me, the
    friend of his youth. Well . . . and so on, and so on . . .
    it's all a matter of give and take. That'll teach you.
    (He takes BROWN by the arm.) Well, Jacky, I'm glad
    you've come. That's what I call real friendship. (A
    pause while BROWN sorrowfully regards a carpet.)
    Genuine Shiraz.
BROWN: From the Oriental Carpet Company.
MACHEATH: We get all our carpets there. Do you know,
    I had to have you here today, Jacky. I hope you don't
    feel too uncomfortable, being in the position you are.

BROWN: You know, Mac, I can't refuse you anything. But
I must be going. I've got so much on my mind. If the
least thing should go wrong at the Coronation . . .

MACHEATH: Jacky, you know my father-in-law is a repulsive old swine. If he were to raise some sort of stink
about me, are there any records in Scotland Yard
that could be used against me?

BROWN: In Scotland Yard there is not the slightest thing
against you, Mac.

MACHEATH: Of course not.

BROWN: I saw to that. Good night.

MACHEATH: Aren't you all going to stand up?

BROWN (*to* POLLY): All the best!

Exit BROWN *accompanied by* MACHEATH.

JACOB (*who meanwhile with* MATTHEW *and* WALTER *has
been conferring with* POLLY): I must admit I couldn't
repress certain trepidations when I heard Tiger Brown
was coming!

MATTHEW: You know, miss, we have our contacts with
the highest authorities.

WALTER: Yes. Mac always has an extra iron in the fire
which the likes of us haven't a glimmering of! But we
have our little irons in the fire too. Gentlemen, it's half
past nine.

MATTHEW: And now — the high spot.

*All retire to the back, behind a hanging carpet which
conceals something.* MACHEATH *enters.*

MACHEATH: What's up now?

MATTHEW: Another little surprise, Captain.

*Behind the carpet they sing "The Wedding Song for
Poorer People," very softly and full of feeling. How-*

ever, when they get to the end of the first verse,
MATTHEW *tears down the carpet and they sing on,*
bawling at the top of their voices and beating time
on a bed which stands behind.

MACHEATH: Thank you, friends, thank you.
WALTER: And now the unobtrusive departure.

The gang exeunt.

MACHEATH: And now sentiment must come into its own,
for otherwise man becomes a mere slave to his work.
Sit down, Polly.

Music.

Do you see the moon over Soho?
POLLY: I see it dearest. Can you feel my heart beating,
beloved?
MACHEATH: I can feel it, beloved.
POLLY: Whither thou goest, I shall go with thee.
MACHEATH: And where thou stayest, there too shall I stay.

Both sing:

MACHEATH:
    And if there's no license or Registrar
    Nor lovely flowers to make you a crown

POLLY:
    And if I don't know exactly who you are
    Or where I got hold of this gown:

BOTH:
    The platter from which you are eating your bread
    Don't you keep it long, throw it down
    For love lasts forever (or not so long)
    In many and many a town.

3

FOR PEACHUM, WHO KNOWS THE HARDNESS OF THE
WORLD, THE LOSS OF HIS DAUGHTER MEANS NOTHING
LESS THAN TOTAL RUIN

Peachum's Establishment for Beggars

Right, PEACHUM *and* MRS. PEACHUM. *In the doorway
stands* POLLY, *in hat and coat, a small suitcase in her hand.*

MRS. PEACHUM: Married? First we load her fore and aft
with dresses and hats and gloves and parasols, and
when she's cost as much as a sailing ship to rig out,
she flings herself in the gutter like a rotten tomato.
Have you really gone and got married?

> *Song illumination: golden light. The organ is lit up.
> Three lights come down on a bar, and on a board is
> written:*

IN A LITTLE SONG POLLY GIVES HER PARENTS A HINT
OF HER MARRIAGE WITH THE GANGSTER MACHEATH

When I was a girl, and an innocent girl
(I was innocent once as were you)
I thought that perhaps I might interest some fellow
And so I must know just what to do.
And if he's a rich fellow
And if he's a nice fellow
And his collar is as white as snow
And if he knows how he should treat a real lady
Then I must tell him: No.
That way I can hold my head up high
And be a lady comme il faut.
Yes, the moon shines bright until it's day!
Yes, the boat is launched and duly sails away!

And that's just how far things go.
For one must not rush a fellow off his feet!
No, one must be cold and very slow.
For, hey presto, so much might happen!
The only word to use is: No.

The first man who came was a man from Kent
Who was all that a man should be.
The second, oh, he had three schooners in the harbor
And the third one was crazy for me.
And as they were rich men
And as they were nice men
And their collars were as white as snow
And as they knew how they should treat a real lady
I had to say to each one: No.
That way I could hold my head up high
And be a lady comme il faut.
Yes, the moon shone bright till it was day!
Yes, the boat was launched and duly sailed away!
And that's how far things could go.
For one must not rush a fellow off his feet!
No, I must be cold and very slow.
For, hey presto, so much might happen!
But not if I should whisper: No.

And yet one afternoon (and that day the sky was blue)
Came someone who did not ask.
And he hung his bowler hat upon the nail inside my
    bedroom
And applied himself to his task.
And as he was not rich
And as he was not nice
And even his Sunday collar was black as a crow
And as he didn't know how he should treat a real lady
I could not tell him: No.
This way I couldn't hold my head up high

Or be a lady comme il faut.
Oh, the moon shone bright the whole night long
But the boat was tied up good and strong
And it all had to be just so.
For a man must simply rush us off our feet
And one really needn't be so cold or slow.
For, hey presto, it had to happen:
I could not tell that someone No.

PEACHUM: So now she's become a crook's hussy! *Very*
nice. That's lovely.

MRS. PEACHUM: If you're already so immoral as to marry
at all, why must it be a horse thief and a footpad?
That'll cost you dear some day! I should have seen it
coming. Even as a child she had a head as swollen as
the Queen of England.

PEACHUM: So she really got married.

MRS. PEACHUM: Yes. Yesterday afternoon at five o'clock.

PEACHUM: To a notorious criminal! Come to think of it,
it shows great courage in the man. If I have to give
away my daughter, the last support of my old age, my
house will fall in and my last dog will desert me. Why,
I couldn't give away the dirt under my fingernails without risking death from starvation. If the three of us
can get through the winter on one log of wood, we may
live to see next year. We *may*.

MRS. PEACHUM: What are you thinking of? This is our
reward for everything, Jonathan. I shall go mad.
Everything is going round in my head. I can't stand
any more. Oh! *(She faints.)* A glass of brandy!

PEACHUM: There! See what you've done to your mother.
Quick! A crook's trollop, that's fine, that's charming.
Strange how the old lady has taken it to heart.

POLLY *returns with a bottle of brandy.*

The last consolation left for your poor mother!

POLLY: Go on, you can give her two glasses. *My* mother can carry twice as much when she's not herself. That'll put her on her legs again. *(During the whole of this scene she has a radiantly happy expression on her face.)*

MRS. PEACHUM *(revives)*: Oh! Now she's showing her wicked false sympathy and solicitude again!

Five men enter.[5]

BEGGAR: I must complain most strongly. Because this place is a pigsty. Because this isn't a proper stump, but just a mess, and I won't waste my money on it.

PEACHUM: What do you want? It's as good as the others, only you don't keep it clean.

BEGGAR: All right — then why don't I earn as much as the others? No, you can't put that over on me. *(Hurls the stump away.)* I might as well cut off my real leg, if I wanted such junk.

PEACHUM: Well, what *do* you want? What can *I* do about it if people have hearts of granite. I can't make you five stumps! In ten minutes I can make such a wreck out of any man that a dog would howl if he saw him. What can I do if *people* won't howl? There, take another stump, if one's not enough for you. But look after your things.

BEGGAR: That'll have to do.

PEACHUM *(tries a false arm on another beggar)*: Leather is no good, Celia. Rubber is more repulsive. *(To the third:)* The bruise is going down, and it's your last. Now we can start all over again. *(Examining the fourth.)* Of course, natural scabs are never the same as artificial ones. *(To the fifth:)* What's happened to you? You've been eating again. You'll have to be made an example of.

BEGGAR: Mr. Peachum, I really haven't eaten much, my fat's unnatural, I can't help it.

PEACHUM: Neither can I. You're dismissed. *(Turning his back to the second beggar.)* Between "giving people a shock" and "getting on their nerves" there's obviously a difference, my friend. I need artists. Today, only artists give people the right sort of shock. If you'd work properly, your public would be forced to appreciate you. But that never occurs to you. So naturally I cannot extend your engagement.

The beggars exeunt.

POLLY: Please consider him. Is he handsome? No. But he makes a living. He offers me an existence. He's a first-class burglar, a farsighted and experienced street robber. I could tell you exactly what he's got saved up. A few more successful enterprises and we can retire to a little house in the country, just like that Mr. Shakespeare father admires so much.

PEACHUM: Well then, it's all quite simple. You're married. What do you do when you're married? Don't bother to think. You get a divorce. Eh? Is that so hard to arrange?

POLLY: I don't know what you mean.

MRS. PEACHUM: Divorce.

POLLY: But I love him, how can I think of divorce?

MRS. PEACHUM: Polly, aren't you ashamed of yourself?

POLLY: Mother, if you've ever been in love . . .

MRS. PEACHUM: Love! Those damned books you've been reading have turned your head. Polly, *everyone* does it!

POLLY: Then I shall be an exception.

MRS. PEACHUM: I'll beat your bottom, you exception!

POLLY: All mothers do that, but it's no use. Because love is greater than a beaten bottom!

MRS. PEACHUM: Polly, don't try my patience too far.

POLLY: I won't let you rob me of my love!

MRS. PEACHUM: Another word, and you'll get a box on the ears.

POLLY: Love is the greatest thing in the world!

MRS. PEACHUM: And that fellow has several women. When he's hanged, there'll be half a dozen of them reporting as widows, each probably with a brat in her arms. — Oh, Jonathan!

PEACHUM: Hanged! How did you come to think of hanging? It's a good idea! Go outside, Polly.

Exit POLLY.

You're right. The idea's worth forty pounds.

MRS. PEACHUM: I know what you mean. Tell the sheriff.

PEACHUM: Of course. Besides, this way we get him hanged free. . . . It'll be two birds with one stone. Only we've got to find out where he's hiding.

MRS. PEACHUM: I can tell you, my dear. He's with his whores.

PEACHUM: But they won't give him up.

MRS. PEACHUM: Leave it to me. Money rules the world. I'll go straight to Wapping and talk to the girls. If this fine gentleman meets a single one of them two hours from now, he's a goner.

POLLY *(who has been listening behind the door)*: My dear Mama, you can save yourself the trouble. Before Mac would speak to such a woman, he'd give himself up to the police. And if he went to the police, the Sheriff would offer him a cocktail, and over a cigar they'd discuss a certain business in this street where things aren't quite as they should be either. For, dear Papa, the Sheriff was very merry at my wedding.

PEACHUM: What's the name of this Sheriff?

POLLY: His name is Brown. But you'd only know him as Tiger Brown. Because all who are afraid of him call him Tiger Brown. But my husband, you see, calls him Jacky. They were boyhood friends.

PEACHUM: I see, they're friends, are they? The Sheriff and the number one criminal. Then they're probably the only friends in this fine city.

POLLY (rhapsodically): Whenever they had a cocktail together, they'd stroke each other's cheek and say, "If you'll have another, I'll have another." And whenever one went out, the other's eyes grew moist and he'd say, "Whither thou goest, I will go too." There's nothing against Mac in Scotland Yard.

PEACHUM: I see. Between Tuesday evening and Thursday morning, Mr. Macheath — surely a much married gentleman — has enticed my daughter Polly Peachum from her parental home under the pretext of marriage. Before this week is over, this will be sufficient to bring him to the death he so richly deserves. "Mr. Macheath, you once had white kid gloves and a stick with an ivory handle and a scar on your neck and you frequented the Octopus Hotel. All that remains is your scar, the least valuable of your distinguishing marks, and henceforth you will frequent only prison cells, and soon you won't frequent anywhere . . ."

MRS. PEACHUM: Oh, Jonathan, you'll never succeed, for it's Mackie the Knife you're dealing with. They say he's the greatest criminal in London. He takes what he wants.

PEACHUM: Who is Mackie the Knife? Polly, get ready, we're going to the Sheriff of London. And *you're* going to Wapping.

MRS. PEACHUM: To his whores.

PEACHUM: For the wickedness of the world is so great you

have to run your legs off to avoid having them stolen
from under you.

POLLY: And I, Papa, will be very glad to shake Mr. Brown
by the hand again.

*All three walk to the front of the stage and to song
illumination sing the first finale. On the board is
written:*

FIRST THREEPENNY-FINALE
ON THE UNCERTAINTY OF HUMAN CIRCUMSTANCES

POLLY:

> There's a thing I want to try:
> Once in this my dark existence
> To reward a man's persistence.
> Do you think I aim too high?

PEACHUM *(with a Bible in his hands)*:

> The right to happiness is fundamental:
> Men live so little time and die alone.
> Nor is it altogether incidental
> That they want bread to eat and not a stone.
> The right to happiness is fundamental.
> And yet how great would be the innovation
> Should someone claim and get that right — hooray!
> The thought appeals to my imagination!
> But this old world of ours ain't built that way.

MRS. PEACHUM:

> How I wish I could supply
> Philanthropical assistance
> To relieve your dark existence
> But one must not aim so high.

PEACHUM:

> To be a good man — what a nice idea!
> And give the poor your money? That is fine!

When all mankind is good, His Kingdom's near!
Who would not like to bask in Light Divine?
To be a good man — what a nice idea!
But there's the little problem of subsistence:
Supplies are scarce and human beings base.
Who would not like a peaceable existence?
But this old world is not that kind of place.

POLLY AND MRS. PEACHUM:

I fear he's right, $\begin{cases} \text{my} \\ \text{your} \end{cases}$ dear old dad:
The world is poor and men are bad.

PEACHUM:

Of course, he's right, your dear old dad:
The world is poor and men are bad.
An earthly paradise might be arranged
If this old world of ours could but be changed
But that can never be arranged.
Your brother might be fond of you
But if the meat supply won't do
He'd cut you down right where you stood.
(We'd all be loyal if we could.)
Your good wife might be fond of you
But if your love for her won't do
She'd cut you down right where you stood.
(We'd all be grateful if we could.)
Your children might be fond of you
But if your pension would not do
They'd cut you down right where you stood.
(We'd all be human if we could.)

POLLY AND MRS. PEACHUM:

We do not mind confessing
The whole thing is depressing.
The world is poor and men are bad
And we have nothing more to add.

PEACHUM:

> There is of course no more to add.
> The world is poor and men are bad.
> We would be good, instead of base
> But this old world is not that kind of place.

ALL THREE:

> We take no comfort from your bunk
> For everything's a heap of junk.

PEACHUM:

> The world is poor and men are bad
> There is of course no more to add.

ALL THREE:

> We do not mind confessing
> The whole thing is depressing.
> We take no comfort from your bunk
> For everything's a heap of junk.

ACT TWO

I

THURSDAY AFTERNOON. MACKIE THE KNIFE TAKES LEAVE
OF HIS WIFE BEFORE FLEEING ACROSS HIGHGATE MOOR
TO ESCAPE HIS FATHER-IN-LAW

The Stable

POLLY *(enters)*: Mac! Mac! Don't be afraid, it's me.

MACHEATH *(lying on a bed)*: What's the matter? What are
you looking like that for, Polly?

POLLY: I've just been to see Brown, and my father was
there too, and they're plotting to catch you. My father
threatened something terrible, and Brown stuck up
for you at first; but he gave in later, and he thinks you
ought to disappear for a while. Mac, you must pack
quickly!

MACHEATH: What! Pack? Nonsense! Come here, Polly!
We're going to do something quite different from
packing.

POLLY: No, Mac, we can't now. I'm so frightened. They
were talking about hanging all the time.

MACHEATH: I don't like it, Polly, when you're moody!
There's nothing against *me* in Scotland Yard.

POLLY: No, perhaps there wasn't. But today there's a terrible lot. Listen, I've brought the list of charges with
me. I don't know whether I shall get through it, it's
endless: you've killed two shopkeepers, and committed
more than thirty burglaries, twenty-three street rob-
beries, arsons, attempted murders, forgeries, perjuries
— and all in eighteen months. You're a terrible per-

son, Mac. And in Winchester you seduced two sisters, both under the age of consent.

MACHEATH: They told me they were twenty-one. And what did Brown say?

He stands up slowly and walks to the right along the footlights, whistling.

POLLY: He caught me up in the corridor and said he couldn't do anything more for you. Oh, Mac! *(She throws her arms around his neck.)*

MACHEATH: Well then, if I *must* go, you'll have to take over the business.

POLLY: Don't talk of business now. I can't bear it! Mac, kiss your Polly again and swear that as far as she is concerned you'll never, never . . .

MACHEATH *(interrupts her and leads her to the table, where he pushes her down into a chair)*: These are the account books. Listen carefully. This is a list of the staff. *(Reads.)* Hook-Finger Jacob, a year and a half in business; let's see what he's brought in. One, two, three, four, five gold watches. Not much, but it's good skilled work. — Don't sit on my lap. I'm not in the mood now. And here's Walter — Wally the Weeper — an unreliable swine. Fences stuff on his own account. Three weeks grace for him, then the gallows. Simply report him to Brown.

POLLY *(sobbing)*: Simply report him to Brown.

MACHEATH: Jimmy the Second, an impudent customer — profitable but impudent. Pinches sheets from under the finest female backsides in the land. Give him a rise.

POLLY: I'll give him a rise.

MACHEATH: Robert — call him Robert the Saw — a petty thief without a trace of genius. He won't end on the gallows, he'll never come to anything.

POLLY: Never come to anything.

MACHEATH: Otherwise carry on the same as before: get up at seven, wash, take one bath a day, and so forth.

POLLY: You're right, Mac, I shall just have to set my teeth and keep an eye on the business. What's yours is mine, isn't it, Mackie? But, Mac, what about your rooms? Shall I give them up? I'm horrified at the rent!

MACHEATH: No, I need them.

POLLY: But why? They only cost us money.

MACHEATH: You seem to think I'm never going to come back.

POLLY: What do you mean? You can take them again! [6] Mac . . . Mac, I can't stand it any longer. I look at your lips and I don't hear what you're saying. Will you be true to me, Mac?

MACHEATH: Of course I'll be true to you. I'll repay like with like. Do you think I don't love you? It's just that I look further ahead.

POLLY: I'm so glad, Mac. You think of me when they're after you like bloodhounds . . .

When he hears the word "bloodhounds," MACHEATH *stiffens, stands up, crosses to the right, takes off his coat and starts washing his hands.*

MACHEATH *(hurriedly)*: Send all the profits to Jack Poole's banking house in Manchester. Between ourselves, it's only a question of weeks before I switch to banking exclusively. It's safer as well as more profitable. In two weeks at the most the money must be out of this business. And then you'll go to Brown and hand the whole list of names to the police. In four weeks at the most, all this scum of the earth will be standing their trial at the Old Bailey.

POLLY: But Mac! How can you look them in the eye when you're going to double-cross them like this and have

them as good as hanged? Can you still shake them by
the hand?

MACHEATH: Who? Money Matthew, Hook-Finger Jacob,
Robert the Saw, Wally the Weeper . . . those jailbirds?

Enter the gang.

Gentlemen, I'm very glad to see you.

POLLY: . . . gentlemen.

MATTHEW: Captain, I've got the plans for the Coronation
here. There's a day of good hard work ahead of us.
The Archbishop of Canterbury arrives in half an hour.

MACHEATH: When?

MATTHEW: Five-thirty. We must go at once, Captain.

MACHEATH: Yes, you must go at once.

ROBERT: What do you mean: *you*?

MACHEATH: As far as I'm concerned, I'm afraid I've got
to take a short trip to the country.

ROBERT: What? Are they going to nab you?

MATTHEW: And just when the Coronation's coming off!
A Coronation without you will be soup without a
spoon.

MACHEATH: Shut your mouth. I'm handing over the man-
agement of the business to my wife for a short time.
— Polly! *(He pushes her to the front and then retires
to the back, where he watches her.)*

POLLY: Men, I think our Captain can go away without
having to worry. We shall get along fine, eh?

MATTHEW: I've got nothing to say. But I don't know if a
woman . . . at a time like this . . . I'm not saying
anything against *you*, ma'am . . .

MACHEATH *(from the back)*: What do you say to that,
Polly?

POLLY: You've made a good start, you son of a bitch!
(Screaming.) Of course you're not saying anything
against me, or these gentlemen here would long ago

have had your trousers off and tanned your bottom. Isn't that so, gentlemen?

A short pause, then they all clap like mad.

JACOB: She's all right!

WALTER: Bravo! Our new captain knows the answers! Hurrah for Polly!

ALL: Hurrah for Polly!

MACHEATH: It's a shame I can't be in London for the Coronation. It'll be a gold mine. Every house empty during the day, and at night all the best people drunk. That reminds me, Matthew — you drink too much. Last week you made it obvious that it was you that set fire to the children's hospital at Greenwich. If this happens again, you're sacked. Who set fire to the children's hospital?

MATTHEW: I did.

MACHEATH *(to the others)*: Who set it on fire?

THE FIVE OTHERS: You did, Captain.

MACHEATH: Who did?

MATTHEW *(sullenly)*: You did. This way, the likes of me will never come up in the world.

MACHEATH *(with a gesture of hanging)*: You'll come up all right, if you try to compete with me. Did you ever hear of an Oxford professor letting all his scientific mistakes be made by some assistant? Of course not: he takes the credit for them himself.

ROBERT: Ma'am, now you're in command while your husband's away . . . payday every Thursday, ma'am.

POLLY: Every Thursday, men!

Exit gang.

MACHEATH: And now, good-bye, my love. Keep fresh, and don't forget to make up every day, just as if I were there.

POLLY: And you, Mac, promise me you'll never look at another woman, and that you'll leave London at once. Believe me, your little Polly doesn't say this out of jealousy, but because it's important.

MACHEATH: But, Polly, why should *I* bother with second-hand goods? I love only you. When it's dark enough I shall start out, get my black stallion from . . . oh, some stable or other, and before you can see the moon from your window, I shall be far beyond Highgate Moor.

POLLY: Oh, Mac, don't tear my heart from my body. Stay with me and let us be happy.

MACHEATH: But I have to tear my own heart from my body, for I have to go and no one knows when I shall return.

POLLY: It lasted such a little while, Mac.

MACHEATH: And now it is over?

POLLY: Mac, last night I had a dream. I was looking out of the window and I heard laughter in the street, and when I looked up I saw our moon, and the moon was quite thin, like a penny that's all worn away. Don't forget me, Mac, in the strange cities.

MACHEATH: Of course I shall never forget you, Polly. Kiss me, Polly.

POLLY: Good-bye, Mac.

MACHEATH: Good-bye, Polly. *(As he exits:)*

> For love lasts forever (or not so long)
> In ever so many a town.

POLLY *(alone)*: And he never will come back again! *(She sings:)*

> Sweet while it lasted
> And now it is over.
> Tear out your heart
> Say "Good-bye, good Polly!"
> What use is your weeping

(Blessed Virgin, restore me)
When it's plain my mother
Knew all this before me!

The bells ring.

The Queen is now in London on her way.
Where shall we be on Coronation Day?

INTERLUDE

MRS. PEACHUM *and* GINNY JENNY *step out in front of the curtain.*

MRS. PEACHUM: So if you see Mackie the Knife in the next few days, run to the nearest copper and report him. You'll get ten shillings for it.

GINNY JENNY: But do you think we'll see him if the police are after him? When the hunt starts, he won't be wasting any time with us.

MRS. PEACHUM: Let me tell you this, Jenny: if all London were after him, Macheath is not the man to give up his old habits.

She sings:

THE BALLAD OF SEXUAL SUBMISSIVENESS*

Now here's a man who fights old Satan's battle:
The butcher, he! All other men, mere cattle!
He is a shark with all the world to swim in!

---

* The German title, *Ballade der Sexuellen Hörigkeit*, smacks of Krafft-Ebing, but the equivalent phrases in Havelock Ellis's *Psychology of Sex* — "erotic slavery" and "erotic servitude" — refer to a disease decidedly different from the one diagnosed by Mrs. Peachum. I have therefore chosen a word that is closer to the phenomenon described.

The meter of the refrains is that of the Weill score and not that of the German lyrics as published in the *Stücke*. — E.B.

What gets him down? What gets 'em all down? Women.
He may not want to, but he'll acquiesce
For such is sexual submissiveness.
He does not heed the Bible nor the Statute Book.
He says he is an egomaniac.
If women look at him, he won't look back
For girls can murder with a look.
His fortitude by daylight is surprising
But when the night is falling, he is rising.

And many saw the tragic fall of many:
The great Macheath fell into Harlot Jenny.
Those who stood by might swear his sins were scarlet
But when they died, who buried them? Some harlot.
They may not want to, but they acquiesce
For such is sexual submissiveness.
Some read the Bible; others take a Law Degree;
Some join the Church and some attack the State;
While some remove the celery from their plate
And then devise a theory.
By evening all are busy moralizing
But when the night is falling, they are rising.

2

THE CORONATION BELLS HAVE NOT YET RUNG OUT AND
MACKIE THE KNIFE IS ALREADY AMONG HIS WHORES AT
WAPPING. THE GIRLS BETRAY HIM. IT IS THURSDAY EVENING

A Brothel in Wapping

*An ordinary evening. The whores, mostly in their shifts,
are quietly ironing, playing draughts, washing themselves:
a middle-class idyll.*[7] JENNY *sits alone on one side.* HOOK-

FINGER JACOB *is reading the newspaper without anyone paying the slightest attention to him. In fact, he is rather in the way.*

JACOB: He won't come today.

WHORE: Won't he?

JACOB: I don't think he'll *ever* come again.

WHORE: That would be a pity.

JACOB: Would it? If I know him, he's out of the city by this time. Up and away!

Enter MACHEATH. *He hangs his hat on a nail and sits on the sofa behind the table.*

MACHEATH: My coffee, please!

VIXEN *(repeats astounded)*: "My coffee, please!"

JACOB *(horrified)*: Why aren't you in Highgate?

MACHEATH: Today is Thursday. I cannot let such trifles disturb my habits. *(He throws his charge-sheet on the floor.)* Besides, it's raining.

GINNY JENNY *(reads the charge-sheet)*: "In the name of the Queen, Captain Macheath is herewith charged with triple . . ."

JACOB *(snatching it from her)*: Am I there too?

MACHEATH: Of course, the whole staff.

GINNY JENNY *(to another whore)*: Look, here are the charges. *(Pause.)* Mac, give me your hand. *(He holds out his hand as he drinks from a coffee cup in the other.)*

DOLLY: Yes, Jenny, read his hand.

She holds forward a paraffin lamp.

MACHEATH: A rich legacy?

GINNY JENNY: No, not a rich legacy.

BETTY: Why are you looking at him like that, Jenny? It's enough to give anyone the shivers.

MACHEATH: A long journey in the near future?

GINNY JENNY: No, not a long journey.

VIXEN: What do you see then?

MACHEATH: Only good news, please! No bad!

GINNY JENNY: Oh well! I see a narrow strip of darkness
there and a little love. And then I see a large T, which
means the treachery of a woman. Then I see . . .

MACHEATH: Stop. I'd like to have a few details about the
narrow strip of darkness and the treachery: for example, the name of the treacherous woman.

GINNY JENNY: I can only see that it begins with J.

MACHEATH: Then it's wrong. It begins with P.

GINNY JENNY: Mac, when the Coronation bells ring out
from Westminster, you'll have a bad time of it.

MACHEATH: Go on. (JACOB laughs raucously.) What's the
matter? (He goes across to JACOB, and reads.) Quite
wrong, there were only three.

JACOB (laughs): That's just it.

MACHEATH: Nice underwear you have here.

WHORE: From the cradle to the coffin, underwear comes
first.

OLD WHORE: I never use silk. The gentlemen immediately
think you're ill.

GINNY JENNY edges stealthily out of the door.

SECOND WHORE (to GINNY JENNY): Where are you going,
Jenny?

GINNY JENNY: You'll see. (Exit.)

MOLLY: But plain linen puts them off.

OLD WHORE: I've had great success with plain linen.

VIXEN: That's because the gentlemen feel at home with it.

MACHEATH (to BETTY): Have you still got the black braid?

BETTY: Yes, still the black braid.

MACHEATH: And what sort of underwear do you have, my
dear?

SECOND WHORE: Oh, I'm so ashamed, I can't bring 'em to my room, my aunt hates men. And in doorways, you know, you just can't have on underwear.

JACOB *laughs.*

MACHEATH: Finished?

JACOB: No, I'm just at the "rapes."

MACHEATH *(again sitting on the sofa)*: But where's Jenny got to? Ladies, long before my star rose over this town . . .

VIXEN: Long before my star rose over this town . . .

MACHEATH: I lived in the poorest circumstances with one of you fair ladies. And though I am Mackie the Knife now, in my present happiness I shall never forget the companions of my darker days: above all Jenny, whom I loved the best of all the girls. Listen!

As MACHEATH *sings,* GINNY JENNY *stands outside the window right and beckons to* CONSTABLE SMITH. *Then* MRS. PEACHUM *joins her. All three stand under the street lamp and look into the house.*

THE BALLAD OF THE FANCY MAN

MACHEATH:

Once on a time — who knows how long ago? —
We shared a home together, I and she.
My head and her abdomen turned the trick.
I protected her and she supported me.
(Some say it's different, but I say it's slick.)
And when a wooer came I crept out of our bed
And got myself a schnapps and showed myself
  well-bred.
When he shelled out, I said: Auf Wiedersehn
If any time you'd care to, come again!

For half a year we had no cause to roam
For that bordello was our home from home.

Enter GINNY JENNY *through the door: behind her,*
SMITH.

GINNY JENNY:

> At that same time — it's rather long ago —
> He took the bloom off our relationship.
> For when the cash was short, he bawled me out.
> One day he yelled: I'm going to pawn your slip!
> (A slip is nice but one can do without.)
> And then — you know how 'tis — I felt a certain
> pique.
> I asked him more than once: how did he have the
> cheek?
> Then he would pummel me, would my good pal
> And I would end up in the hospital.
> Life was all honey from the honeycomb
> In that bordello which was home from home.

BOTH TOGETHER, ALTERNATELY

BOTH: And at that time — long, long, long, long ago —[8]
HE: (To think of it just now gives me a lift)
SHE: By day alone could we two sport and play
HE: For night was usually her working shift.
    (The night is usual, but there's also the day.)
SHE: One day I felt beneath my heart a young Macheath.
HE: We then and there agreed: I should lie underneath.
SHE: An unborn child, you know, so often crushes.
HE: At that, *this* child was destined for the rushes.
BOTH: Though that bordello was our home from home
    In half a year we were constrained to roam.

Dance. MACHEATH *picks up his swordstick: she hands*
him his hat; and he is still dancing when SMITH *lays*
a hand on his shoulder.

MACHEATH: Has this rat hole still got only one exit?

SMITH *attempts to handcuff* MACHEATH. MACHEATH *pushes against his chest, so that he stumbles over backward. Then* MACHEATH *jumps out of the window. But outside are* MRS. PEACHUM *and other policemen.*

MACHEATH *(calmly and very politely)*: Good evening, madam.

MRS. PEACHUM: My dear Mr. Macheath! My husband always says: "The greatest heroes in history have always tripped up over little obstacles."

MACHEATH: May I inquire how your husband is?

MRS. PEACHUM: Better — now. Well, you can take your leave of these ladies. Officers, take Mr. Macheath to his new lodgings. *(He is led off.* MRS. PEACHUM *speaks through the window.)* The gentleman will be living henceforth at the Old Bailey. If you should wish to visit him, ladies, you will always find him at home. I knew he'd be here with his whores! I will settle the bill. Farewell, ladies. *(Exit.)*

GINNY JENNY: Hey Jacob! Something's happened.

JACOB *(who, on account of his intensive reading, has noticed nothing)*: Where's Mac?

GINNY JENNY: The coppers were here!

JACOB: No! And here was I quietly reading . . . boys, boys, boys! *(Exit.)*

3

BETRAYED BY THE WHORES, MACHEATH IS FREED FROM PRISON THROUGH THE LOVE OF ANOTHER WOMAN

Prison in the Old Bailey. A Barred Cage.

Enter BROWN.

BROWN: I hope my men don't catch him! Dear God, I
hope he's beyond Highgate Moor thinking of his old
friend Jacky! But he's thoughtless, like all men. If they
should bring him in now, and he were to look at me
with those faithful friendly eyes, I couldn't stand it.
Thank God, there's a moon: once he's out in the
country, he'll find his way all right. *(Noise outside.)*
What's that? Oh God, they've got him.

MACHEATH *(tied with heavy ropes and guarded by six constables, enters proudly)*: Well, my minions, here we
are again! Back in our old home. *(He sees* BROWN,
who has retreated to the farthest corner of the cell.)

BROWN *(after a long pause, under the fearful gaze of his
former friend)*: Mac, I didn't do it . . . I did everything
I could . . . don't look at me like that, Mac . . . I
can't bear it . . . Your silence is terrible! *(He shouts
at a constable.)* Don't pull at that rope, you swine!
Say something, Mac. Say something to your old friend
Jacky! Lighten his darkness, I beseech you . . .' *(He
rests his head against the wall and weeps.)* He doesn't
think me worth a word. *(Exit.)*

MACHEATH: That miserable Brown! That evil conscience
incarnate! And a creature like that is made Sheriff of
London! Lucky I didn't bawl him out. I'd intended
doing something of the sort. But then I thought a good,
piercing, punishing stare would send the shivers down
his back. It worked. I looked at him and he wept
bitterly. I got that trick from the Bible.

Re-enter SMITH *with handcuffs.*

Well, Mr. Jailer, I suppose those are the heaviest you
could find? With your permission, I should like a more
comfortable pair. *(He takes out his check book.)*

SMITH: Certainly, Captain, we have them here at all

prices. It depends what you want to pay. From one
to ten guineas.

MACHEATH: How much do none cost?

SMITH: Fifty.

MACHEATH (*writes out a check*): The devil of it is, all
that business with Lucy will come out. And when
Brown hears what I've done to his daughter behind
his friendly back, he'll turn into a real tiger for the
first time in his life.

SMITH: You've made your bed: lie on it.

MACHEATH: I'll bet that trollop is waiting outside. I shall
have a fine time from now till the execution.

So, gentlemen, is this what you'd call living?
Take no offence if Mackie disagrees.
While still a babe I heard with grave misgiving:
None but the well-to-do can take at ease.

*Song illumination: golden light. The organ is illumi-
nated. Three lights come down on a bar from above
— and on the board is written:*

THE SECRET OF GRACIOUS LIVING[9]

Great praise is always lavished on great thinkers
Who think of books (but do not think of dinner)
In some old shack where even rats grow thinner —
I can't abide such solitary stinkers!
For Simple Living simply does not pay
And I'd be glad to hear the last of it.
From here to Rome no turtledove or tit
Would live on such a menu for one day.
Let 'em keep their freedom! Let 'em keep their fleas!
Only the well-to-do can take their ease.

Those brave adventurers whose quaint addiction
Is Truth and Freedom in and out of season

And risking their own necks for no good reason
(Materials for adventurous non-fiction):
See how they waste the wintry evenings napping
Then silently with wintry wife to bed
Their solemn thoughts three thousand years ahead
And both their ears agog for cheers and clapping!
Let 'em keep their bravery! I've a better wheeze:
None but the well-to-do can take their ease.

In spring I ask: could there be something to it?
Could not Macheath be great and solitary?
But then the year works round to January
And I reply: My boy, you'll live to rue it.
Poverty makes you sad as well as wise
And bravery mingles danger with the fame.
Poor, lonely, wise and brave — in heaven's name!
Good-bye to greatness! I return the prize
With this my repartee of repartees:
None but the well-to-do can take their ease.

   Enter LUCY.

LUCY: You miserable wretch, you! How can you look me
    in the face after all that has happened between us?
MACHEATH: Lucy, have you no heart? When you see your
    own husband in this condition?
LUCY: My husband! You brute! So you think I know
    nothing about what you've been up to with Miss
    Peachum? I could scratch your eyes out!
MACHEATH: Lucy, seriously, you're not so silly as to be
    jealous of Polly?
LUCY: So you're not married to her, you beast?
MACHEATH: Married! That's a good one! I visit a certain
    house. I talk to her. Now and then I give her a sort
    of kiss, and the silly bitch runs around boasting that
    she's married to me. My darling Lucy, I'll do any-

thing to reassure you; if you really do believe she and I are married — well and good. What more can a gentleman say? He cannot say more.

LUCY: Oh, Mac, I only want to become an honest woman.

MACHEATH: If you think you'll become an honest woman by being married to me — good. What more can a gentleman say?

Enter POLLY.

POLLY: Where's my husband? Oh, Mac, there you are. You needn't be ashamed of me. After all, I am your wife.

LUCY: Oh, you miserable fiend!

POLLY: Mackie in prison! Why didn't you escape across Highgate Moor? You told me you wouldn't go to those women any more. I knew what they'd do to you; but I didn't say anything; I believed you. Mac, I'll stick with you to the death. — Not a word, Mac, not a look. Oh, Mac, think how your Polly's suffering!

LUCY: Oh, the trollop!

POLLY: What's that, Mac? Who is that woman? Tell her who I am. Am I not your wife? Look at me, am I not your wife?

LUCY: You treacherous swine, have you got two wives, you monster?

POLLY: Say something, Mac. Am I not your wife? Haven't I done everything for you? When I entered the state of matrimony I was pure and innocent, you know that. Didn't you hand over the gang to me? And I did everything as we arranged, and I was to tell Jacob to . . .

MACHEATH: If you two would shut your traps for five minutes I could explain the whole thing.

LUCY: No, I will not shut my trap. I can't stand it, it's more than flesh and blood can stand.

POLLY: Yes, my love, it's clear that woman there . . .

LUCY: That woman!

POLLY: . . . that woman has a certain physical priority. At least to all outward appearances, my love. Such aggravation is enough to drive one mad.

LUCY: Aggravation! That's rich! What have you gone and picked up? This dirty slut! So that's your great conquest! That's your beauty of Soho!

Song illumination: a golden light. The organ is lit up. Three lights come down on a bar from above and on a board is written:

THE JEALOUSY DUET

LUCY:

Come right out, Old Soho's beauty queen!
Let me see those legs they call so pretty!
I should delight to recite the praises
Of the fairest figure in our city!
You might, it is true, produce quite an effect on Mackie!

POLLY:

Oh I might? Oh I might?

LUCY:

If the whole idea were not so wacky!

POLLY:

Is that right? Is that right?

LUCY:

He has better things to do

POLLY:

Has he better things to do?

LUCY:

Than to try his hand on you.

POLLY:

> Than to try his hand on me?

LUCY:

> Ha ha ha ha ha, it can't be fun
> To get mixed up with such a one!

POLLY:

> Very well, let's wait and see.

LUCY:

> Very well, let's wait and see.

TOGETHER:

> Polly ⎱
> Lucy ⎰ loves Mac
> I actually adore him.
> He loves me back:
> All other women bore him.
> A man will not dissever
> A bond that lasts forever
> To please some filthy creature!
> Ludicrous!

POLLY:

> Yes, they call me Soho's beauty queen!
> When they see these legs, they call them pretty!

LUCY:

> But do they?

POLLY:

> They all delight to recite the praises
> Of the fairest figure in our city!

LUCY:

> Shit-pot!

POLLY:

> Shit-pot yourself!
> I have, please observe, produced quite an effect on
> Mackie!

LUCY:

> Oh you have? Oh you have?

POLLY:

> And it's you, my dear, who are so wacky!

LUCY:

> So it's me? So it's me?

POLLY:

> Who, if either hand were free

LUCY:

> Who, if either hand were free?

POLLY:

> Would not try that hand on me?

LUCY:

> Would not try that hand on you?

POLLY:

> Ha ha ha ha ha! But as for you
> Who'd dip his spoon in such a stew?

LUCY:

> Very well, let's wait and see.

POLLY:

> Very well, let's wait and see.

TOGETHER:

> Lucy
> Polly loves Mac
> I actually adore him.
> He loves her back:
> All other women bore him.
> A man will not dissever
> A bond that lasts forever
> To please some filthy creature!
> Ludicrous!

MACHEATH: And now, dear Lucy, be calm. This is just a trick of Polly's. She wants to make trouble. They're going to hang me, and she wants to be able to call herself my widow. Really, Polly, this is not the right moment.

POLLY: You have the heart to deny me?

MACHEATH: And you have the heart to chatter about me being married to you? Why, Polly, must you add to my misery? *(Shakes his head reproachfullv.)* Polly, Polly!

LUCY: Really, Miss Peachum, you're making a show of yourself. Quite apart from the fact that it's monstrous of you to excite a poor gentleman in this plight!

POLLY: The simplest rules of decorum, my dear madam, would teach you, I believe, that a person should behave with somewhat more restraint toward a gentleman in the presence of his wife.

MACHEATH: Seriously, Polly, that's really carrying a joke too far.

LUCY: And if you, my good madam, want to start a row in the prison here, I shall find myself compelled to summon a warder to show you the door. I should be sorry to have to do it, Miss Peachum.

POLLY: Mrs.! Mrs.! Mrs. Macheath! Permit me to tell you this — Miss! — these airs don't suit you in the least! My duty compels me to remain with my husband.

LUCY: What do you say to that? What do you say? She won't go! She stands there and waits to be thrown out! Shall I speak more plainly?

POLLY: You — shut your filthy mouth, you slut, or I'll give you a smack in the chops, dear Miss!

LUCY: I'll have you kicked out, Miss Insolence! It's no use mincing words with you. You don't understand delicacy.

POLLY: You and your delicacy! I'm compromising my own dignity! And I'm too good for that . . . I am! *(She weeps loudly.)*

LUCY: Well, look at my stomach, you trollop! Aren't your eyes open yet?

POLLY: Oh! That! I suppose you're hoping to make something out of it? You should never have let yourself in for it, you fine lady!

MACHEATH: Polly!

POLLY *(sobbing)*: This is really too much, Mac, this shouldn't have happened. I just don't know what I shall do!

Enter MRS. PEACHUM.

MRS. PEACHUM: I knew it. She's with her fancy man. Come here this minute, you filthy trollop. When your man's hanged, you can hang yourself with him. A fine way to behave to your poor old mother: she has to come and fetch you out of prison. So, he has two at a time — that Nero!

POLLY: Leave me alone, mama, you don't know . . .

MRS. PEACHUM: Come home this minute!

LUCY: Listen to that, your mama has to tell you how to behave.

MRS. PEACHUM: Quick march!

POLLY: Wait! I must just . . . I must just say something to him . . . really . . . it's very important.

MRS. PEACHUM *(gives her a box on the ears)*: And that's important too — now — quick march.

POLLY: Oh! Mac! *(She is dragged off by* MRS. PEACHUM.*)*

MACHEATH: Lucy, you behaved wonderfully. Of course, I was sorry for her. That's why I couldn't treat the silly bitch as she deserved. You thought at first there was some truth in what she said? Am I right?

LUCY: Yes, I did think so, dearest.

MACHEATH: Had it been true, her mother would never have got me into this mess. A mother behaves like that only to a seducer, never to a son-in-law.

LUCY: It makes me so happy, when you speak like that from the heart. I love you so much, I'd almost rather see you hanged than in the arms of another girl. Isn't it extraordinary?

MACHEATH: Lucy, I'd like to owe my life to you.

LUCY: It's wonderful, the way you say that. Say it again!

MACHEATH: Lucy, I'd like to owe my life to you.

LUCY: Shall I escape with you, dearest?

MACHEATH: Well, it'll be difficult to hide if we escape together. But as soon as the search is over, I'll have you fetched — by express post, too, as you can imagine!

LUCY: How can I help you?

MACHEATH: Bring me my hat and stick.

LUCY *exits and returns with his hat and stick and throws them into his cell.*

MACHEATH: Lucy, the fruit of our love which you carry beneath your heart will forever bind us together.

Exit LUCY.

SMITH *enters, goes into the cage and says to* MAC-HEATH:

SMITH: Give me that stick.

After a short chase in which SMITH, *armed with a chair and crowbar, drives* MACHEATH *before him,* MACHEATH *leaps over the bars. Constables pursue him.*

BROWN *(off)*: Hello, Mac! Mac, please answer! It's Jacky. Mac, please be kind and answer, I can't beaı it! *(Enters.)* Mackie! What's up? He's gone. Thank God! *(He sits down on the bench.)*

Enter PEACHUM.

PEACHUM *(to* SMITH*)*: My name is Peachum. I have come to claim the forty pounds reward offered for the capture of the bandit Macheath. *(He appears in front of the cage.)* Hey! Is that Mr. Macheath there?

BROWN *remains silent.*

Ah! So the other gentlemen has gone out for a little walk? I come here to visit a criminal and whom do I find but Mr. Brown! Tiger Brown in, and his friend Macheath out.

BROWN *(groaning)*: Mr. Peachum, it's not my fault.

PEACHUM: Of course not, how could it be? You would never be so . . . as to get yourself into this situation . . . would you, Brown?

BROWN: Mr. Peachum, I am beside myself.

PEACHUM: I believe you. You must feel horrible, Brown.

BROWN: Yes, this feeling of helplessness is crushing. The boys do just what they like! It's terrible, terrible!

PEACHUM: Wouldn't you like to lie down a little? Just shut your eyes and behave as though nothing had happened. Imagine you're lying in a lovely green meadow with little white clouds overhead. The main thing is to get this nasty affair out of your mind. Everything that's happened, and above all what's still to come.

BROWN *(uneasily)*: What do you mean?

PEACHUM: It's wonderful the way you're taking it. If I were in your position, I'd simply collapse and go to bed and drink hot tea. And I'd arrange to have a nice cool hand stroking my forehead.

BROWN: Damn you! I can't help it if a man escapes! The police can't do anything!

PEACHUM: Oh! So the police can't do anything. You don't think we shall have Mr. Macheath back here again?

BROWN *shrugs his shoulders.*

Then what's going to happen to you, Brown, will be a horrible injustice. Of course, people will say that the police shouldn't have let him escape. — No, I can't quite see that brilliant Coronation procession yet.

BROWN: What do you mean?

PEACHUM: I might remind you of an historic instance, which, although it aroused considerable excitement in its time, fourteen hundred years B.C., is unknown to the larger public of today. When the Egyptian king Rameses the Second died, the chief of police of Nineveh, or it may have been Cairo, was guilty of some petty injustice toward the lower classes. Even at that time the results were terrible. The coronation procession of the new queen, Semiramis, was, as the history books state, "a succession of catastrophes caused by the all too lively participation of the lower classes." The historians are far too squeamish to describe what Semiramis had done to her chief of police. I only remember vaguely; but there was talk of snakes which she nourished at his bosom.

BROWN: Really?

PEACHUM: The Lord be with you, Brown. *(Exit.)*

BROWN: Now only an iron hand will do any good! Sergeant, a conference! Emergency!

Curtain. MACHEATH *and* GINNY JENNY *step in front of the curtain and sing. Song illumination.*

SECOND THREEPENNY-FINALE

MACHEATH:

Now all you gentlemen who wish to lead us
Who teach us to desist from mortal sin
Your prior obligation is to feed us:
When we've had lunch, your preaching can begin.
All you who love your paunch and our propriety
Take note of this one thing (for it is late):

You may proclaim, good sirs, your fine philosophy
But till you feed us, right and wrong can wait!
Or is it only those who have the money
Can enter in the land of milk and honey?

VOICE OFF:

What does a man live by?

MACHEATH:

What does a man live by? By resolutely
Ill-treating, beating, cheating, eating some
    other bloke!
A man can only live by absolutely
Forgetting he's a man like other folk!

CHORUS OFF:

So, gentlemen, do not be taken in:
Men live exclusively by mortal sin.

GINNY JENNY:

All you who say what neckline is decreed us
And who decide when ogling is a sin
Your prior obligation is to feed us
When we've had lunch, your preaching can begin.
You who insist upon your pleasure and our shame
Take note of this one thing (for it is late):
Your fine philosophy, good sirs, you may proclaim
But till you feed us, right and wrong can wait!
Or is it only those who have the money
Can enter in the land of milk and honey?

VOICE OFF:

What does a man live by?

GINNY JENNY:

What does a man live by? By resolutely

Ill-treating, beating, cheating, eating some
    other bloke!
A man can only live by absolutely
Forgetting he's a man like other folk!

CHORUS OFF:

So, gentlemen, do not be taken in:
Men live exclusively by mortal sin.

ACT THREE

1

THE SAME NIGHT PEACHUM PREPARES FOR ACTION. BY MEANS OF A DEMONSTRATION OF MISERY HE HOPES TO DISORGANIZE THE CORONATION PROCESSION

The Wardrobe Room of Peachum's Establishment

The beggars are painting boards with such inscriptions as "I gave my eye for my king," etc.

PEACHUM: Gentlemen, at this very hour, in our eleven branches between Drury Lane and Wapping, there are one thousand four hundred and thirty-two men like you working on such boards as these in order to be present at the Coronation of our Queen.

MRS. PEACHUM: Come on, come on! If you won't work, you can't beg. You hope to be a blind man, and you can't even write a proper K! That's supposed to be a child's handwriting, not an old man's!

> *Exit PEACHUM.*
> *Roll of drums.*

BEGGAR: There's a guard of honor lining up! Little do they dream that today, the grandest day of their military lives, they've got to deal with us!

FILCH (*enters and announces*): Here comes a dozen benighted birds, Mrs. Peachum. They say they're to be given their money here.

> *Enter the whores.*

GINNY JENNY: My dear madam . . .

MRS. PEACHUM: Well, well, well, you look as though you've all fallen off your perches! I suppose you've come for the money for your Macheath? You'll get nothing. Understand? Nothing.

GINNY JENNY: And what are we to understand by that, madam?

MRS. PEACHUM: Bursting into my room in the middle of the night! Coming to a respectable house at three in the morning! You'd do better to sleep off the effects of business. You look like skim milk.

GINNY JENNY: So we're not to get our contractual fee for having Mr. Macheath nabbed, madam?

MRS. PEACHUM: Quite correct. In fact, you'll get something you don't like, instead of your blood money.

GINNY JENNY: And why, madam?

MRS. PEACHUM: Because your wonderful Mr. Macheath has vanished again into thin air. That's why. Now get out of my decent house, ladies.

GINNY JENNY: That's the limit. Don't you try that on with us! I give you fair warning, not with us!

MRS. PEACHUM: Filch, the ladies want to be shown out.

FILCH *approaches the girls.* GINNY JENNY *pushes him away.*

GINNY JENNY: I'd advise you to keep your dirty mouth shut . . . or!

Enter PEACHUM.

PEACHUM: What's the matter? I hope you haven't given them any money. Well, what's the matter, ladies? Is Mr. Macheath in prison or is he not?

GINNY JENNY: Leave me in peace with your Mr. Macheath. You're not a patch on him. I had to send a gentleman away tonight because I wanted to cry on my pillow every time I thought how I had sold that real gentleman to you. Yes, ladies, and what do you think happened this morning? Not an hour ago, when I had just cried myself to sleep, I heard a whistle, and there in the street below stood the gentleman I'd been crying for, and he asked me to throw the key down to him: he wished to forget the wrong I had done him — in my arms. He's the last gentleman left in London, ladies. And if our colleague Suky Tawdry isn't with us now, it's because he went from me to her, to comfort her as well.

PEACHUM *(to himself)*: Suky Tawdry . . .

GINNY JENNY: So now you know. You're dirt compared to him. You lowdown informers!

PEACHUM: Filch, run quickly to the nearest police station and say Mr. Macheath is staying with Miss Suky Tawdry.

Exit FILCH.

But ladies, why are we quarreling? Your money will be paid, of course. My dear Celia, wouldn't it be better if you went and made the ladies a nice cup of coffee, instead of insulting them?

MRS. PEACHUM: Suky Tawdry!

She sings the third verse of the "Ballad of Sexual Submissiveness."

Now here's a man who toward the gallow races.
The quicklime's bought that will rub out his traces.
He's dead the minute hangmen do their duty.
And what's his mind on now, this chap? Some beauty.
Here at the gallows' foot he'll acquiesce
For such is sexual submissiveness.

He's had it. He's been sold. He marches to his doom.
He's seen the money in a female's hand
And he begins to understand
That woman's orifice will be his tomb.
His self-reproaches are uncompromising
But, as the night is falling, he is rising.

Exit MRS. PEACHUM.

PEACHUM: Come on, come on! You'd all be rotting in the
sewers of Wapping if I hadn't spent sleepless nights
working out how to extract a few pence from your
poverty. And I did work out something: that the rich
of the earth indeed create misery, but they cannot
bear to see it. They are weaklings and fools just like
you. As long as they have enough to eat and can grease
their floors with butter so that even the crumbs that
fall from their tables grow fat, they can't look with
indifference on a man collapsing from hunger — although, of course, it must be in front of *their* house
that he collapses.

Re-enter MRS. PEACHUM *with a tray full of coffee
cups.*

MRS. PEACHUM: You can come to the shop tomorrow and
fetch your money: but *after* the Coronation.
GINNY JENNY: Mrs. Peachum, you leave me speechless.
PEACHUM: Fall in! We assemble in an hour outside Buck-
ingham Palace. Quick march!

The beggars fall in.

FILCH (*bursts in*): The coppers! I never got as far as the
station. The coppers are here already!
PEACHUM: Hide yourselves. (*To* MRS. PEACHUM:) Get
the orchestra ready! And when you hear me say
"harmless," understand me, *harmless* . . .

MRS. PEACHUM: Harmless? I don't understand a thing.

PEACHUM: Of course you don't understand a thing. So when I say "harmless" . . .

There is a knocking on the door.

Thank God, that's the password, *harmless,* then play some sort of music. Now get out.

Exit MRS. PEACHUM. *The beggars, excepting a girl with the board* A VICTIM OF MILITARY DESPOTISM, *hide with their things behind the clothes racks on the right.*

Enter BROWN *with constables.*

BROWN: And now, Mr. Beggars' Friend, we take action! Handcuff him, Smith. Ah, so those are a few of your charming notices. *(To the girl:)* "A Victim of Military Despotism" — is that you, my dear?

PEACHUM: Good morning, Brown, good morning. Slept well?

BROWN: Eh?

PEACHUM: Morning, Brown.

BROWN: Is he speaking to me? Does he know any of you? I don't think I have the pleasure of your acquaintance.

PEACHUM: Haven't you? Morning, Brown.

BROWN: Knock his hat off, Smith.

SMITH *does so.*

PEACHUM: Listen, Brown, since your way leads *past* my house — I said *past,* Brown — I can now ask you to put a certain Macheath under lock and key.

BROWN: The man is mad. Smith, stop laughing. Tell me, Smith, how is it possible that this notorious criminal is allowed at large in London?

PEACHUM: Because he's your friend, Brown.

BROWN: Who?

PEACHUM: Mackie the Knife. Not me, I'm not a criminal. I'm just a poor man, Brown. You can't treat me badly. Listen, Brown. You are on the verge of the worst hour of your life. Would you like a cup of coffee? *(To the whores:)* Girls, give the gentleman a drink, that's not the way to behave. We're all friends here. We all obey the law. The law is simply and solely made for the exploitation of those who do not understand it or of those who, for naked need, cannot obey it. And whoever would pick up the crumbs of this exploitation must strictly obey the law.

BROWN: You think our judges are bribable?

PEACHUM: On the contrary, sir, on the contrary! Our judges are totally unbribable: no amount of money can bribe them to dispense justice.

A second roll of drums.

Departure of the troops to line the route! Departure of the poorest of the poor half an hour later!

BROWN: Quite right, Mr. Peachum. Departure of the poorest of the poor in half an hour. They're departing for their winter quarters in prison. *(To the constables:)* Well, boys, round 'em up. All the patriots you can find here. *(To the beggars:)* Have you ever heard of Tiger Brown? Tonight, Mr. Peachum, I have found the solution and, I may add, I have saved a friend from death. I shall simply smoke out your whole nest. Then I shall lock you all up for — yes, what *for*? For street-begging! You seem to have warned me that you were going to bother me and the Queen with your beggars. These beggars I shall now arrest. That'll teach you something.

PEACHUM: All very fine — but what beggars?

BROWN: These cripples here. Smith, we'll take the patriotic gentlemen with us right away.

PEACHUM: Brown, I can save you from overstepping your duty. Thank God you came to me! Of course you can arrest these few people, they are *harmless, harmless . . .*

Music starts and plays a few introductory bars of "The Song of the Futility of all Human Endeavor."

BROWN: What's that?

PEACHUM: Music. They play as well as they can. "The Song of Futility." Don't you know it? That'll teach you something!

Song illumination: golden light. The organ is lit up. Three lights come down from above on a bar, and on a board is written:

THE SONG OF THE FUTILITY OF ALL HUMAN ENDEAVOR

> A man lives by his head.
> That head will not suffice.
> Just try it: you will find your head
> Will scarce support two lice.
>> For the task assigned them
>> Men aren't smart enough or sly.
>> Any rogue can blind them
>> With a clever lie.
>
> Go make yourself a plan
> And be a shining light.
> Then make yourself a second plan
> For neither will come right.
>> For the situation
>> Men aren't bad enough or vile.
>> Human aspiration
>> Only makes me smile.

Go running after luck
But don't you run too fast:
We all are running after luck
And luck is running last.
  For the real conditions
  Men are more demanding than is meet.
  Their ideal ambitions
  Are one great big cheat.

PEACHUM: Your plan was ingenious, Brown, but imprac-
ticable. All you can arrest here are a few young people
who arranged a small fancy-dress ball to celebrate the
Coronation of their Queen. But when the really poor
ones come — there's not a single one here now —
you'll see they'll come in thousands. That's the trouble.
You've forgotten the monstrous number of the poor.
If they were to stand there in front of the Abbey, it
wouldn't be a very cheerful sight. They don't look
very nice. Do you know what erysipelas is, Brown?
Well, think now of a hundred people with erysipelas
on their faces. And then these mutilated creatures at
the door of the Abbey? We would rather avoid that,
Brown. You say the police will make short work of
us poor people. But you don't believe it yourself.
What will it look like if six hundred poor cripples have
to be knocked down with your truncheons because of
the Coronation? It will look bad. Enough to make
one sick. I feel ill, Brown, just to think of it. A chair,
please.

BROWN (to SMITH): This is a threat. It's blackmail. We
can't do anything to this man. In the interest of the
public order we can't do anything to this man. Such a
thing has never happened before!

PEACHUM: It has happened now, Brown. I'll tell you something: you can do what you like to the Queen of England, but just try and tread on the toes of the poorest man in London and we'll do you brown, Mr. Brown.

BROWN: Then I'm to arrest Mackie the Knife? Arrest him? You can talk! You've got to catch your man before you can arrest him.

PEACHUM: When you say that, I cannot contradict you. So I shall produce him for you. We'll see if there's any morality left! Jenny, where is Mr. Macheath staying?

GINNY JENNY: With Suky Tawdry, at 621 Oxford Street.

BROWN: Smith, go at once to 621 Oxford Street, Suky Tawdry's flat, arrest Macheath and bring him to the Old Bailey. In the meantime I must change into my full-dress uniform. On occasions like this, I have to wear full dress.

PEACHUM: Brown, if he's not hanged by six . . .

BROWN: Oh, Mackie, it didn't work. (*Exit* BROWN *with constables.*)

PEACHUM (*calling after him*): That's taught you something, Brown.

A third roll of drums.

Drums — the third time! A fresh plan of campaign! New destination: the Old Bailey! Quick march!

Exeunt the beggars.

PEACHUM (*sings*):
>Since men are just no good
>Pick up a piece of wood
>And hit them on the head with it!
>Then maybe they'll be good.

For the human function
They'll be good when they are dead.
So without compunction
Hit them on the head!

In front of the curtain appears GINNY JENNY *with a hurdy-gurdy. She sings:*

THE SONG OF SOLOMON

King Solomon was very wise
So what's his history?
He came to view this world with scorn
And curse the hour he was born
Declaring all is vanity.
King Solomon was very wise
But long before the day was out
The consequence was clear, alas!
And wisdom 'twas that brought him to this pass:
A man is better off without.

You saw Queen Cleopatra too
And what her talents were.
Oh, it was quite a life she led
Until her past caught up with her!
Two emperors joined her in bed:
Such goings-on in Babylon!
But long before the day was out
The consequence was clear, alas!
Her very beauty brought her to this pass:
A woman's better off without.

And Julius Caesar: he was brave.
His fame shall never cease.
He sat like God on an altarpiece
And then they tore him limb from limb
And Brutus helped to slaughter him.

Old Julius was very brave
But long before the day was out
The consequence was clear, alas!
His bravery 'twas that brought him to this pass:
A man is better off without.

You know the inquisitive Bertolt Brecht.
His songs — you loved them so.
But when too oft he asked where from
The riches of the rich did come
You made him pack his bag and go.
Oh how inquisitive was Brecht!
But long before the day was out
The consequence was clear, alas!
Inquisitiveness had brought him to this pass:
A man is better off without.

And here you see our friend Macheath.
His life is now at stake.
So long as he was rational
And took whate'er there was to take
His fame was international.
But then he got emotional
And though the day is not yet out
The consequence is clear, alas!
Emotion 'twas that brought him to this pass:
A man is better off without.

2

THE BATTLE FOR POSSESSION [10]

An Attic Bedroom in the Old Bailey

SMITH: Miss, Mrs. Polly Macheath would like to speak
to you.

LUCY: Mrs. Macheath? Show her in.

Enter POLLY.

POLLY: Good morning, madam. Madam, good morning!

LUCY: What can I do for you?

POLLY: You recognize me again?

LUCY: Of course I recognize you.

POLLY: I've come to beg pardon for my behavior yesterday.

LUCY: Very interesting.

POLLY: I have no excuse at all for my behavior yesterday, except — my unhappiness.

LUCY: I see.

POLLY: You must forgive me. I was very upset yesterday by Mr. Macheath's behavior. He really shouldn't have placed us in such a position, don't you agree? You can tell him so, when you see him.

LUCY: I — I — don't see him.

POLLY: You *do* see him.

LUCY: I do *not* see him.

POLLY: I'm sorry.

LUCY: He is very fond of you.

POLLY: Oh no, he loves you, I know that all right.

LUCY: You're very kind.

POLLY: But a man always fears a woman who loves him too much. And the natural result is that he neglects that woman and avoids her. I saw at first glance that he was bound to you in some way which I naturally couldn't guess.

LUCY: Do you mean that, honestly?

POLLY: Certainly. Of course. Very honestly.

LUCY: Dear Miss Peachum, we have both loved him too much!

POLLY: Perhaps that was it. *(Pause.)* And now, I'll explain how it came about. Ten days ago I saw Mr. Macheath for the first time in the Octopus Hotel. My mother was there too. Later — that is, the day before yesterday — we were married. Yesterday I discovered the police wanted him for a great many crimes. And today I don't know what will happen. So you see, twelve days ago I wouldn't have dreamed I could ever fall for a man. *(Pause.)*

LUCY: I quite understand, Miss Peachum.

POLLY: Mrs. Macheath.

LUCY: Mrs. Macheath.

POLLY: And, indeed, during the last few hours I have been thinking a lot about this fellow. It's not so simple. For, you see, Miss Brown, I have every reason to envy you his behavior toward you the other day. When I had to leave — coerced, I must admit, by my mama — he showed not the slightest regret. But perhaps he hasn't got a heart, just a stone in its place. What do you think, Lucy?

LUCY: Dear Miss Peachum, I am not quite sure if the fault lies entirely with Mr. Macheath. Perhaps you should have kept to your own sort, Miss Peachum.

POLLY: Mrs. Macheath.

LUCY: Mrs. Macheath.

POLLY: You're quite right — or at least I ought to have kept everything, as my father says, "on a business basis."

LUCY: Of course.

POLLY *(weeps)*: He is all that I have.

LUCY: My dear, this is a misfortune that can happen to the cleverest woman. But you are legally his wife, comfort yourself with that. Child, I can't bear to go on seeing you so depressed. May I offer you a little something?

POLLY: A little what?

LUCY: A little something to eat?

POLLY: Oh, yes, please! A little something to eat!

Exit LUCY.

(To herself:) The silly little fool!

LUCY *(returning with coffee and cakes)*: Now that'll be enough.

POLLY: You really give yourself too much trouble. *(Pause. She eats.)* A lovely picture you have of him. When did he bring it?

LUCY: What do you mean — bring it?

POLLY: *(innocently)*: I meant, when did he bring it up here.

LUCY: He didn't bring it.

POLLY: Didn't he give it to you right here in this room?

LUCY: He never was in this room.

POLLY: I see. But there would have been nothing in that. The paths of fate are already terribly complicated!

LUCY: Don't talk such tripe all the time. You came here to spy around!

POLLY: You know where he is, don't you?

LUCY: I? Don't *you* know?

POLLY: Tell me where he is this minute!

LUCY: I haven't the slightest idea.

POLLY: Then you don't know where he is? Word of honor?

LUCY: No, I don't. And you don't know either?

POLLY: No! This is monstrous! *(POLLY laughs and LUCY weeps.)* He has two responsibilities now and he's run out on both of us!

LUCY: I can't bear it any longer. Oh, Polly, it's so awful!

POLLY *(happily)*: But I'm so glad that at the ending of this
tragedy I've found a friend like you. Have some more?
Another cake?

LUCY: Some more! Oh, Polly, don't be so kind to me.
Really I don't deserve it! Oh, Polly, men aren't worth
it!

POLLY: Of course men aren't worth it. But what can one
do?

LUCY: I'll come clean. Will you be angry with me, Polly?

POLLY: What?

LUCY: It's not real.

POLLY: What isn't?

LUCY: This! *(She points to her stomach.)* I did it all for
that crook!

POLLY *(laughs)*: It was a trick. Wonderful! You are a little
fool! Listen — you want Mackie? I'll give him to you.
Take him when you find him.

There is a sound of voices and steps outside.

What's that?

LUCY *(at the window)*: It's Mackie! They've caught him
again.

POLLY *(collapses)*: Then all is over!

Enter MRS. PEACHUM.

MRS. PEACHUM: Ah, Polly, so here you are. Change your
dress. Your husband's going to be hanged. I've
brought your widow's weeds.

POLLY *starts to undress and puts on the widow's
weeds.*

You'll look lovely as a widow! Now cheer up a bit.

3

5 A.M. FRIDAY. MACKIE THE KNIFE, WHO ONCE MORE
WENT BACK TO HIS WHORES, HAS AGAIN BEEN BETRAYED
BY THEM. HE IS NOW ABOUT TO BE HANGED

The Death Cell

The bells of the City are ringing. Constables bring MAC-
HEATH, *handcuffed, into the cell.*

SMITH: In here with him. The bells have rung once already. *(To Macheath:)* Try and behave like a man. I
don't know how you manage to look so washed out. I
should think you must be ashamed of yourself! *(To
the other constables:)* When the bells ring for the third
time — that'll be at six o'clock — he must be already
hanged. Get everything ready.

A CONSTABLE: Every street in Newgate has been jammed
with people for the last quarter of an hour. It's impossible to get through.

SMITH: Extraordinary! How do they know already?

CONSTABLE: If it goes on like this, the whole of London
will know in half an hour. Those who were going to
the Coronation will all come here instead. The Queen
will have to drive through empty streets.

SMITH: That's why we shall have to hurry. If we're
through by six, people can be back on the Coronation
route by seven. Get on with it.

MACHEATH: Hi, Smith! What's the time?

SMITH: Haven't you got eyes? Four minutes past five.

MACHEATH: Four minutes past five.

As SMITH *shuts the door of the cell from the outside,*
BROWN *enters.*

BROWN *(questioning* SMITH, *with his back to the cell)*: Is
he there?

SMITH: You want to see him?

BROWN: No, no, no, for God's sake, manage it all yourself.
(Exit.)

MACHEATH *(suddenly bursting into a soft and rapid tor-
rent of speech)*: Listen, Smith, I won't say a thing, not
a thing, about bribery, don't worry. I know all about
that. If you let yourself be bribed, you'll at least have
to get out of the country. You'd have to do that. And
you'll also need money to live on for the rest of your
life. A thousand pounds, will that do? Don't speak!
In twenty minutes I'll let you know if you can have
that thousand pounds by midday. I'm not mentioning
anyone's feelings. Go outside and think it over carefully. Life is short and so is money. And I'm not sure
I can raise any. But let anyone in here who wants to
see me.

SMITH *(slowly)*: You're talking nonsense, Mr. Macheath.
(He withdraws to the side of the stage.)

MACHEATH *(sings, softly and very quickly)*:
Hark to the voice that pleads for pity, hark!
Macheath lies here — beneath no hawthorn tree
Nor under elms but in a dungeon dark.
He was struck down by angry Fate's decree.
God grant you all may hear what he doth say!
Him thickest walls surround and chains entwine.
Do you not ask, my friends, where he hath strayed?
When he is dead, brew elderberry wine!
But while he still doth live, lend him your aid.
Or must his martyrdom endure for aye? [11]

MATTHEW *and* JACOB *appear in the passage.* SMITH
intercepts them on their way to MACHEATH.

SMITH: We-e-ll, my boys! You look like a gutted herring!

MATTHEW: Now the Captain's away, it's I who have to get the ladies pregnant — so, when they're arrested, they can plead "Not responsible for their actions." One needs the physique of a stallion for this job. Can I speak with the Captain?

SMITH *lets them pass, then exit.*

MACHEATH: Five twenty-five. You've taken your time.

JACOB: Well, after all . . .[12]

MACHEATH: After all, after all, I'm going to be hanged, man! But I've no time to argue with you. Five twenty-eight. How much can you draw out of your private deposits immediately?

MATTHEW: At five o'clock in the morning?

JACOB: Is it really as bad as all that?

MACHEATH: Four hundred pounds? Can you manage that?

JACOB: Well, and what about us? That's all there is.

MACHEATH: Are you going to be hanged, or am I?

MATTHEW (*excitedly*): Did we sleep with Suky Tawdry instead of making ourselves scarce? Did we sleep with Suky Tawdry or did you?

MACHEATH: Shut your gob. I'll soon be sleeping somewhere else than with that trollop. Five thirty.

JACOB: I suppose we'll have to do it, Matthew.

SMITH (*enters*): Mr. Brown told me to ask what you'd like for — breakfast.

MACHEATH: Leave me alone! (*To* MATTHEW:) Will you or won't you? (*To* SMITH:) Asparagus.

MATTHEW: I'm certainly not going to be shouted at!

MACHEATH: I'm not shouting at you! It's only because . . . Now, Matthew, are you going to let me be hanged?

MATTHEW: Of course we won't let you be hanged. Whoever suggested that? But that's all. Four hundred pounds is all there is. One's allowed to say that, I suppose.

MACHEATH: Five thirty-eight.

JACOB: Hurry, Matthew, or it'll be too late.

MATTHEW: If we can only get through. The streets are jammed. This riff-raff!

MACHEATH: If you're not here by five minutes to six, you'll never see me again. (*Shouts.*) You'll never see me again . . . !

SMITH: They're off. Well, how goes it? (*He makes a gesture of paying out money.*)

MACHEATH: Four hundred.

SMITH *walks away, shrugging his shoulders.*

MACHEATH (*calling after him*): I must speak to Brown.

SMITH (*as the constable enters*): You've got the soap?

CONSTABLE: It's not the right sort.

SMITH: You'll be able to set the thing up in ten minutes.

CONSTABLE: But the trap isn't working yet.

SMITH: It *must* work, the bells have rung the second time.

CONSTABLE: This is a hell of a place!

MACHEATH (*sings*):

> Alas, he's fallen from his high estate.
> All his affairs have gone from bad to worse.
> Oh ye who recognize nor God nor Fate
> But place your bets upon your own fat purse
> You'd better rescue him or, well-a-day,
> He'll drag you all down to that dungeon grim.
> Run then unto the Queen for your Macheath.
> Tell her the pass he's come to. Say of him:
> That man of sorrows, Queen, has fangs for teeth.
> Or must his martyrdom endure for aye?

Enter POLLY.

SMITH: I can't let you in. Your number's sixteen. It's not your turn yet.

POLLY: What do you mean: my number's sixteen? I am his wife. I must speak to him.

SMITH: Then five minutes at the most.

POLLY: What do you mean, five minutes! That's ridiculous. Five minutes! You just can't say that. It's not as simple as all that. This is good-bye forever. And there's such a lot that has to be said between man and wife . . . Where is he?

SMITH: Well, can't you see him?

POLLY: Oh yes. Thank you!

MACHEATH: Polly!

POLLY: Yes, Mackie, here I am.

MACHEATH: Yes, of course.

POLLY: How are you? Very done up? It's hard.

MACHEATH: Yes, and what will *you* do? What will become of you?

POLLY: Oh, our business is doing very well. That's the least of our troubles. Mackie, are you very nervous? Who *was* your father? There's so much you haven't told me. I don't understand it at all: you were really always quite healthy.

MACHEATH: Polly, can't you help me out?

POLLY: Of course.

MACHEATH: With money, I mean. I talked to the warder here . . .

POLLY (*slowly*): The money has gone to Southampton.

MACHEATH: And you haven't any?

POLLY: No, I haven't any. But do you know, Mac, perhaps I could speak to someone . . . maybe the Queen herself! (*She breaks down.*) Oh, Mackie!

SMITH (*pulling* POLLY *away*): Got your thousand pounds?

POLLY: Good luck, Mac, take care of yourself! Never forget me! (*Exit.*)

SMITH *and a constable bring on a table with a plate of asparagus on it.*

SMITH: Is the asparagus tender?

CONSTABLE: It is. *(Exit.)*

BROWN *enters and walks over to* SMITH.

BROWN: What does he want, Smith? I'm glad you waited for me with the table. We'll take it with us, so he'll see what consideration we have for him. *(They both carry the table into the cell. Exit* SMITH. *Pause.)* Hello, Mac. Here's your asparagus. Won't you try a little?

MACHEATH: Don't trouble yourself, Mr. Brown, there are other people who will do me the last honors.[18]

BROWN: But Mackie!

MACHEATH: I should like the account! Forgive me if, in the meanwhile, I eat. After all, this is my last meal. *(He eats.)*

BROWN: Good appetite! Oh, Mac, you wound me as with a red-hot iron!

MACHEATH: The account, sir, please! No sentimentality.

BROWN *(sighing, draws a little notebook out of a pocket)*: I have brought it, Mac. Here is the account for the last six months.

MACHEATH *(scathingly)*: I see. So you've only come to get your money out of me.

BROWN: Mac, you know that's not true . . . !

MACHEATH: All right, you shan't be the loser. What do I owe you? But please let me have a detailed statement. Life has made me mistrustful . . . And you're the one who ought to know why.

BROWN: Mac, when you speak like that, I can't think straight.

There is a loud banging behind.

SMITH (off): All right, that will hold.

MACHEATH: The account, Brown.

BROWN: Very well — if you insist, there are the rewards for the arrests you or your people made possible. You received from the Government in all . . .

MACHEATH: Three murderers at forty pounds each makes a hundred and twenty pounds. A quarter of that for you is thirty pounds, which we owe you.

BROWN: Yes — yes — but I really don't know, Mac, at the last minute, as it were, if we can . . .

MACHEATH: Please cut out the slop. Thirty pounds. And the one in Dover eight pounds.

BROWN: But why only eight pounds, for there was . . .

MACHEATH: Do you believe me or do you not? So for the last half year there's thirty-eight pounds due to you.

BROWN (sobbing loudly): A life-time together . . . I knew your every thought . . .

BOTH: . . . by just looking in your eyes.

MACHEATH: Three years in India — Johnny and James were both on the scene — five years in London and this is all the thanks I get. (He shows what he will look like when hanged.)

> Here hangs Macheath who ne'er a soul did wrong:
> A former friend his former friend betrays.
> And hanging by a rope a fathom long
> His neck can tell him what his bottom weighs.

BROWN: Mac, if you're going to treat me like this . . . ! Who attacks my honor attacks me! (He runs angrily out of the cage.)

MACHEATH: Your honor?

BROWN: Yes, my honor! Smith, begin! Let the people in! (To MACHEATH:) Excuse me, please.

SMITH (entering hurriedly, to MACHEATH): I can still get

you away, but in one minute it'll be too late. Have
you got the money?

MACHEATH: Yes, as soon as the boys get back.

SMITH: There's no sign of them. Well — that's off.

People are admitted: PEACHUM, MRS. PEACHUM,
POLLY, LUCY, *the whores, the* REVEREND KIMBALL,
MATTHEW *and* JACOB.

GINNY JENNY: They didn't want to let us in, but I told
them: if you don't take your something heads out of
my way, you'll get to know Ginny Jenny better than
you like!

PEACHUM: I am his father-in-law. Pardon me, which of
those present is Mr. Macheath?

MACHEATH *(presents himself)*: Macheath.

PEACHUM *(walks past the cage)*: Fate, Mr. Macheath, has
decreed that you should become my son-in-law without my knowing you. The circumstances in which I
meet you for the first time are very tragic. Mr. Macheath, you once had white kid gloves, a stick with an
ivory handle, and a scar on your neck, and you frequented the Octopus Hotel. There remains the scar
on your neck, which is probably the least valuable of
your distinguishing marks, and now you only frequent
jails, and very soon you won't frequent anywhere . . .

POLLY *walks sobbing past the cage and stands right.*

MACHEATH: What a pretty dress you're wearing.

MATTHEW *and* JACOB *come past the cage and stand
right.*

MATTHEW: We couldn't get through because of the crowd.
But we ran so fast I thought Jacob was going to have
a stroke. If you don't believe us . . .

MACHEATH: What do the men say? Have they got good places?

MATTHEW: There, Captain, we knew you'd understand. Look, we don't get a Coronation every day. The men have to earn when they can. They ask to be remembered to you.

JACOB: Kindly.

MRS. PEACHUM (*walks past the cage and stands right*): Mr. Macheath, who would have thought of this when a week ago we had a little dance together at the Octopus Hotel?

MACHEATH: Yes, a little dance.

MRS. PEACHUM: But here on earth below Fate is cruel.

BROWN (*to the* REVEREND KIMBALL *at the back*): And with this man I stood at Azerbaijan, shoulder to shoulder, under withering fire!

GINNY JENNY (*comes to the cage*): Us Drury Lane girls are in a terrible fix. Not a soul's gone to the Coronation; they all want to see you. (*She stands right.*)

MACHEATH: To see me.

SMITH: Come on! Six o'clock. (*He lets him out of the cage.*)

MACHEATH: We will not keep the people waiting. Ladies and gentlemen, you see here the vanishing representative of a vanishing class. We bourgeois artisans, who work with honest jimmies on the cash boxes of small shopkeepers, are being swallowed up by large concerns backed by banks. What is a picklock to a bank share? What is the burgling of a bank to the founding of a bank? What is the murder of a man to the employment of a man? Fellow citizens, I herewith take my leave of you. I thank you all for coming. Some of you have been very close to me. That Jenny should have given me up astonishes me greatly. It is a clear

proof that the world will always be the same. The con-
currence of several unfortunate circumstances has
brought about my fall. Good — I fall.

Song illumination: golden light. The organ is lit up.
Three lights come down from above on a bar and on
a board is written:

BALLAD IN WHICH MACHEATH BEGS PARDON OF ALL

All you who will live long and die in bed
Pray harden not your hearts against us others
And do not grin behind your beards, my brothers,
When you behold us hung till we are dead.
Nor do not curse because we came a cropper.
Be not, as was the Law to us, unkind:
Not every Christian has a lawful mind.
Your levity, my friends, is most improper.
O brother men, let us a lesson be
And pray to God that He may pardon me.

And now the stormwinds with the rain conspire
To wash the flesh we once did overnourish
And ravens gouge our eyes out with a flourish,
These eyes which see so much and more desire.
We were not always virtuous, alas,
That's why you'll see us hanging by the neck
For every greedy bird of prey to peck
As were we horses' offal on the grass.
So, brother men, let us a warning be
And pray to God that He may pardon me.

The wenches with their bosoms showing
To catch the eye of men with yearnings
The urchins just behind them going
In hopes to filch their sinful earnings

The outlaws, bandits, burglars, gunmen
All Christian souls that love a brawl
Abortionists and pimps and fun-men
I cry them mercy one and all.

Except the coppers — sons of bitches —
For every evening, every morning
Those lice came creeping from their niches
And frequently without a warning.
Police! My epidermis itches!
But for today I'll let that fall
Pretend I love the sons of bitches
And cry them mercy one and all.

O, I could smash their ugly faces
And crush them with an iron maul!
But one can't always hold the aces.
I cry them mercy one and all.

SMITH: If you please, Mr. Macheath.

MRS. PEACHUM: Polly and Lucy, stand by your husband in his last hour.

MACHEATH: Ladies, whatever may have been between us . . .

SMITH (*leads him off*): Come on!

PASSAGE TO THE GALLOWS

All exeunt through the doors left. These doors are set in the wings. Then they re-enter from the other side of the stage, all carrying hurricane lamps. When MACHEATH *is standing on the gallows,* PEACHUM *speaks.*

PEACHUM:

So, gentlemen, to this point we have come.
You all can see what Captain Mackie's fate is.
Which proves that in the whole of Christendom
Nothing is granted any of us gratis.

But lest you jump to the conclusion
That we are parties to the deal, and in collusion,
Macheath will *not* be hanged till he is dead.
We have devised another end instead.

You all will hear (yes, all; it's rather loud)
Mercy give Justice quite a dreadful hiding.
This is an opera, and we mean to do you proud.
The Royal Messenger will make his entrance — riding.

On the board is written:

THE ARRIVAL OF THE MOUNTED MESSENGER

THIRD THREEPENNY-FINALE

CHORUS:
    Hark, who comes?
    The Royal Messenger riding comes!

Riding high, BROWN *enters as the messenger.*

BROWN *(recitative)*: On the occasion of her Coronation, our Gracious Queen commands that one Captain Macheath shall at once be released. *(All cheer.)* At the same time he is raised to the permanent ranks of the nobility. *(Cheers.)* The castle of Marmarel and a pension of ten thousand pounds a year are his as long as he shall live, while to all happy couples here our great Queen presents her very cordial congratulations.

MACHEATH: A rescue! A rescue! I was sure of it. Where the need is greatest, there will God's help be nearest.

POLLY: A rescue! A rescue! My dearest Mackie has been rescued. I am so happy

MRS. PEACHUM: So, now the whole thing has a happy end! How calm and peaceful would our life be always if a messenger came from the king whenever we wanted.

PEACHUM: Therefore all remain standing where you are now and sing the chorale of the poorest of the poor, of whose difficult life you have shown us something today. In reality their end is generally bad. Mounted messengers from the Queen come far too seldom, and if you kick a man he kicks you back again. Therefore never be too eager to combat injustice.

All sing to the organ and walk forward.

Combat injustice but in moderation:
Such things will freeze to death if left alone.
Remember: this whole vale of tribulation
Is black as pitch and cold as any stone.

NOTES TO *THE THREEPENNY OPERA*

THE READING OF DRAMAS

JOHN GAY'S own motto for his *Beggar's Opera* was "Nos haec novimus esse nihil" — and there is no reason to change it for *The Threepenny Opera*. As far as the printed version of *The Threepenny Opera* is concerned, it offers little more than the promptbook of a play already wholly delivered over to the theater, and therefore it is addressed to the expert rather than to the reader who merely wants to be amused. Though I must add that the transformation of the greatest possible number of spectators or readers into experts is desirable — and is in fact going on all the time.

The Threepenny Opera deals with bourgeois conceptions, not only as *content* by representing them, but also by the *way* in which they are presented. It is a sort of summary of what the spectator in the theatre wishes to see of life. Since however he sees, at the same time, certain things that he does not wish to see and thus sees his wishes not only fulfilled but also criticized (he sees himself not as a subject, but as an object), he is, in theory, able to give the theatre a new function. But since the theatre itself is resisting the transformation of its function it is a good thing if those dramas whose purpose is not only to be produced in the theatre but also to change the theatre are read by the spectator himself — out of sheer mistrust of the present-day theatre! Today the theatre exerts an absolute primacy over dramatic writing. The primacy of the theatrical apparatus is a primacy of means

of production. The theatre as a whole resists any attempt
to change its function for other ends. The moment it
gets hold of a play, the theatre immediately starts trans-
forming it — except those passages which are not in direct
contradiction to the theatre — so that it no longer in any
way remains a foreign body in the theatre. The necessity
for presenting the new drama adequately — more important for the theatre than for the drama — is weakened
by the fact that the theatre can present anything and
everything: it "theatricalizes" any play. Of course, this
primacy has economic grounds.

TITLES AND BOARDS

The boards on which the titles of the scenes are projected
are a primitive start toward a *literarization of the theatre*.
This literarization of the theatre, as indeed the literarization of all public affairs, must be developed to the greatest
possible extent.

Literarization means putting across ideas through actions; interspersing the "performed" with the "formulated."
It makes it possible for the theatre to establish contact
with other institutions of intellectual activity, but it must
remain a one-sided affair so long as the audience does not
take part in such literarization and thus breaks through
to "higher things."

From the standpoint of orthodox dramatic art, it can be
said against the titles that the playwright should be able
to say everything he has to say through the play itself,
that the work ought to be able to express everything in-
trinsically. This corresponds to a spectator's attitude of
mind in which he does not think about the matter, but
from within the matter. However, this way of subordinat-
ing everything to an idea, this urge to drive the spectator
into a single-track dynamism whence he can look neither

right nor left, up nor down, must be rejected from the standpoint of modern dramatic art. In drama, too, we should introduce footnotes and the practice of thumbing through and checking up.

Complex seeing must be practiced. Though thinking *about* the flow of the play is more important than thinking from *within* the flow of the play. Besides which, the boards compel and enable the actors to achieve a new style. This style is the *epic style*. In reading the projections on the boards the spectator takes up the attitude of one who smokes at ease and watches. By such an attitude the spectator immediately forces from the actor a better and fairer performance; for it is hopeless to attempt to "spellbind" a man who is smoking and who is therefore pretty well preoccupied with himself. By this means we would very quickly have a theatre full of experts, just as there are sports arenas full of experts. It would be impossible for the actors to fob off such an audience with a few wretched bits of attitudinizing that are put on "any old how" nowadays, with a minimum of rehearsals and without the least thought. Never would the public accept the actors' material in such a raw state and so unfinished. Since every action has already been deprived of its intrinsic power to surprise by the caption title on the boards, the actors are forced to make it striking by entirely different means.

Unfortunately, it is to be feared that captions and permission to smoke will not suffice entirely to bring the public to a more productive use of the theatre.

THE CHIEF CHARACTERS

The character of Jonathan Peachum must not be presented as the conventional recipe for a "skinflint." Money means nothing to him. To him, who mistrusts everything which might arouse hope, even money appears to be a wholly inadequate defense. He is undoubtedly a villain, and indeed a villain in the convention of the old-fashioned theatre. His crime consists in his conception of the world, and this, in all its atrociousness, is worthy to stand beside the accomplishments of any of the world's other great criminals; yet he is only following the "trend of the times" when he regards misery as a commodity. In actual practice, Peachum would never lock up in his till the money he takes from Filch in the first scene; he would simply push it into his trouser pocket; neither this money nor any other can save him. It is pure conscientiousness on his part, and proves his general despair, that he does not simply throw it away. He cannot throw the least thing away. He would think no differently if it were a matter of a million shillings. In his view neither his money (nor all the money in the world), nor his brains (nor all the brains in the world) are of any use. This is also the reason why he does not work, but runs round his office with his hat on his head and his hands in his pockets, just checking that nothing goes astray. No truly frightened person works. It is not petty of him when he chains the Bible to the lectern for fear it may be stolen. He never looks at his son-in-law until he has brought him to the gallows, since no personal value of any sort could conceivably induce him to adopt a different attitude toward a man who deprives him of his daughter. Macheath's other crimes are only of interest to him inasmuch as they offer a means of disposing of him. As regards his daughter, she is like the Bible — nothing but an expedient. The effect of this is shattering rather than repellent, if one reflects on the degree of desperation where none of the things of this world are of any use except that tiny fraction which might possibly save a foundering man.

The actress who plays Polly will do well to study the foregoing characteristics of Mr. Peachum. She is his daughter.

The gangster Macheath should be presented by the actor as a bourgeois phenomenon. The predilection of the bourgeois for gangsters is explained by a fallacy: that a gangster is not a bourgeois. Is there then no difference between them? Yes: a gangster is often no coward. The association of "peaceable," which is attached to the bourgeois on the stage, is established by the revulsion of Macheath, the businessman, from the spilling of blood when it is not — for business purposes — strictly necessary. The restriction of bloodshed to a minimum, its rationalization, is a business principle; in an emergency Macheath gives proof of exceptional swordsmanship. He knows what he owes to his reputation; a certain romantic aura, if care is taken to have it talked about, serves the above-mentioned rationalization. He takes the greatest care to insure that all the boldest or, at least, the most fear-inspiring deeds of his subordinates are ascribed to himself; and will not tolerate, any more than a university professor, that his assistants should sign an opus themselves. He strikes women far less as a handsome man than as a comfortably situated man. The original English drawings for *The Beggar's Opera* show a squat but thickset man in his forties, with a head like a radish, already somewhat bald, but not without dignity. He is thoroughly staid, has not the least sense of humor, and his solid respectability is expressed by the mere fact that his commercial activity is aimed not so much at robbing strangers as at exploiting his own employees. With the guardians of public order he is on good terms, even though this costs money, and this not only for reasons of his own safety — for his practical commonsense tells him that his safety and the

satety of this society are intimately bound up together.
An action against public order such as that with which
Mr. Peachum threatens the police would arouse the deep-
est abhorrence in Mr. Macheath. Certainly from his point
of view, his intercourse (social and otherwise) with the
ladies of Wapping requires an excuse; but this excuse is
provided by the peculiar nature of his business. Occasionally he has taken the opportunity of exploiting purely
business transactions for the purpose of amusement to
which, as a bachelor, he is, in moderation, entitled; but
so far as this intimate side of his life is concerned, he
values his regular and pedantically punctual visits to a
certain coffee-house chiefly because these are *habits*
which it is almost the main objective of his bourgeois life
to cultivate and increase.

At all events, the actor who plays Macheath must not,
on any account, choose these visits to a house of ill-fame
as a starting point for his characterization. This is one
of the not rare, yet inexplicable, cases of bourgeois
daemonism.

Of course, in a narrower sense, Macheath prefers to
satisfy his sexual requirements in places where he can
combine them with certain domestic comforts, that is,
with women who are not quite impecunious. In his marriage he sees a means of safeguarding his business. Tem-
porary absence from the metropolis, little as he may value
that absence, is made inevitable by his profession; and
his employees are very unreliable. Looking toward his
own future, he never for a moment envisages himself on
the gallows, only on a peaceful and private stretch of
fishing of his own.

Brown, the Chief of Police, is a very modern phenomenon. He conceals within himself two persons — the
private individual being entirely different from the official.
And this is not a dichotomy *in spite of* which he lives,

but one *because of* which he lives. And besides him, the whole society lives through this dichotomy of his. As a private individual he would never lend himself to what he considers to be his duty as an official. As a private individual he could not (and must not) hurt a fly . . . So his affection for Macheath is thoroughly genuine; certain commercial advantages which spring from it cannot cast a slur on his affection. It is Life that soils everything . . . .

TIPS FOR ACTORS

So far as the communication of the subject matter is concerned, the spectator must not be misled along the path of empathy; instead, a form of intercourse takes place between the spectator and the actor, and basically, in spite of all the strangeness and detachment, the actor addresses himself directly to the spectator. In doing this the actor must tell the spectator more about the "character" he is representing than appears in the actual lines of his part. He must, of course, adopt such an attitude as accommodates the action. But he must also be able to establish relationships with actions other than those of the story, that is, not only those that further the story. For example, in a love scene with Macheath Polly is not only his mistress, but also Peachum's daughter; and, moreover, not only her father's daughter, but also his employee. Her relations with the spectator must contain (within themselves) her own criticism of the spectator's common conceptions about gangsters' brides and merchants' daughters and so forth.

1. The actors should avoid representing these bandits as a gang of those wretched-looking individuals with red neckerchiefs who frequent saloons and with whom no respectable person would drink a glass of beer. They are naturally staid people, some of them portly and all of them sociable outside their profession. (p. 15)

2. Here the actors can display the usefulness of bourgeois virtues and the intimate connection between emotion and crookedness. (p. 15)

3. This scene should demonstrate the brutal energy a man has to exert in order to create a condition in which behavior worthy of a human being (that of a bridegroom) is possible. (p. 16)

4. What must be shown here is the exhibition of the bride, of her carnality, at the moment of final withdrawal from circulation. That is, at the time when supply must cease, demand must once again be driven to the peak. The bride being generally desired, the bridegroom thereupon "sweeps the board." This is a truly theatrical situation. The fact that the bride eats very little must also be stressed. How often does one see the daintiest creatures devouring whole chickens and fishes — but brides never. (p. 20)

5. In demonstrating such things as Peachum's business, the actors need not bother too much about the ordinary development of the plot. However, they must not show a milieu; they must show an incident. The person who takes the part of one of these beggars must endeavor to show the act of selecting a suitable and effective wooden leg (he tries one, lays it aside, examines another and then goes back to the first) in such a manner that for this "turn" alone people will decide, at the time it is taking place, to visit the theatre again to see it, and it is no hindrance if the theatre announces this "number" on a board in the background. (p. 35)

6. It is most desirable that Miss Polly Peachum should impress the audience as a virtuous and agreeable girl. If, in the second scene, she has shown her entirely disinterested love, now she displays that practical outlook without which the aforementioned would have been mere vulgar frivolity. (p. 44)

7. These ladies are in undisturbed possession of their means of production. But for that very reason they must not give the impression of being free. For them, democracy does not grant that freedom which it does to all those from whom the means of production can be taken away. (p. 49)

8. Actors playing the part of Macheath, who display no inhibitions while performing the death struggle, usually refuse at this point to sing the third verse. Of course, they would not reject a tragic presentation of sex but in our day sex undeniably belongs to the realm of comedy, for the sexual life stands in contradiction to social life, and this contradiction is comic because it is historically resolvable, i.e., by a different social order. Therefore the actor must put such a ballad across comically. The stage representation of sexual life is very important, just because a certain primitive materialism always goes with it. The artificiality and transience of all social superstructures becomes apparent. (p. 53)

9. This ballad, like other ballads in *The Threepenny Opera,* contains some lines from François Villon. (p. 56)

10. This scene is inserted for those impersonators of Polly who have a gift for comedy. (p. 79)

11. Running round in a circle in the cage, the actors representing Macheath can repeat all the gaits which he has hitherto displayed to the audience. The cheeky strut of the seducer, the dejected slouch of the hunted, the arrogant walk, the walk of one who has learned his lesson, etc. In this brief peregrination he can once again show all of Macheath's attitudes during the previous few days. (p. 85)

12. At this point, for example, the actor of the epic theatre will not strain to overemphasize Macheath's fear of death and make it the dominant theme of the whole act, thus causing the subsequent scene depicting true

friendship to go by the board. (True friendship is certainly only *true* when it is limited. The moral victory of two of Mr. Macheath's truest friends is, indeed, scarcely diminished by the chronologically later moral defeat of those two gentlemen when they do not make *sufficient* haste to relinquish their means of existence in order to rescue their friend.) (p. 86)

13. Perhaps the actor may here find an opportunity of conveying the following: Macheath has the utterly proper feeling that his case is one of a gross miscarriage of justice. In fact, justice would completely forfeit all respect if *bandits* fell victim to it more frequently than they do! (p. 89)

ON SINGING THE SONGS

When he sings, the actor accomplishes a change of function. Nothing is more detestable than when an actor gives the impression of not having noticed that he has left the ground of plain speech and is already singing. The three levels — plain speech, heightened speech and singing — must always remain separate from one another, and never can heightened speech be an intensification of plain speech, nor singing of heightened speech. Therefore, in no circumstances will singing take over where words fail for excess of emotion. The actor must not only sing but show a man who is singing. He does not attempt so much to project the emotional content of his song (can one offer others food which one has already eaten?) as to display gestures which are, so to speak, the customs and usages of the body. To this end, he would do well, when studying his part, to use not the words of the text, but common current forms of speech which express similar meanings in the everyday idiom. So far as the melody is concerned, he need not follow it blindly; there is a way of speaking-against-the-music which can be very effective just because of an obstinate matter-of-factness, independent of and incorruptible by the music and rhythm. If he drops into the melody, this must be an event; to emphasize this, the actor can show clearly his own delight in the melody. It is a good thing for the actor if the musicians are visible during his recitation, and also good if he is allowed to make visible preparations for his recitations (e.g., arranging a stool or making himself up, etc.). Particularly with a song, it is important that the actual process of performance should be visible as such.

WHY IS MACHEATH ARRESTED TWICE AND NOT ONCE?

This first prison scene is, from the point of view of the German pseudoclassical theatre, a *digression,* but in our view it is an example of primitive epic form. It is only a digression if, as in the case of this purely dynamic drama where primacy is given to the idea and the spectator is made to desire a more and more precise objective — in this case the death of the hero; if there is created an ever increasing demand for the supply (so to speak), and if, in order to bring about a strong feeling of participation on the part of the spectator — (feelings will only trust themselves on completely sure ground and will tolerate no kind of disappointment) — there is a compulsion for the action to proceed in a straight line. *The epic drama having a materialistic approach* has little interest in gripping the feelings of its audience, recognizes indeed no objective, only an end of the play, and knows a different driving force — one whereby the course of action can proceed not only in a straight line but also in curves and even in leaps. The dynamic, idealistically orientated drama, concentrating on the individual, was in all decisive respects more radical when it began its career (with the Elizabethans) than, two hundred years later, under German pseudoclassicism where the driving force of the presentation is substituted for the driving force of the subject, and the individual has been "put in his place." (Their present-day great-great-descendants are beyond comment: the dynamics of representation have meanwhile developed into an empirically arrived at, slick arrangement of a mass of effects, and the individual, now in the course of complete dissolution, is being increasingly fulfilled and made into mere acting parts — whereas the late-bourgeois novel at least worked out the principles of psychology, so it believed, in order to be able to analyze the individual — as if the individual had not long ago disintegrated.) But this grand Elizabethan theatre was less radical in rooting out materialism. Here the construction did not do away with the deviations of the individuals from their straight line, which deviations are caused "by life" — (everywhere there are other extraneous influences being exerted by off-stage circumstances — a much wider swath is cut . . .) — but it used these deviations as dynamic motive forces for forwarding the action. This irritation deeply affects the individual himself, and in him it is overcome. The whole power of this kind of drama comes from the accumulation of resistances. It is not yet the desire for a cheap, ideal formula that determines the arrangement of the material. Herein exists something of Baconian materialism, and the individual, too, still has flesh and blood and struggles against the formula. Everywhere, however, where materialism exists epic forms arise in the realm of drama, generally and most frequently in comedy, whose approach is more materialistic and "lower." Today, when the human being must be regarded as "the totality of all social relationships," the epic form is the only one which can comprise all those processes which provide the dramatist with material for a rounded picture of the world. Even man, carnal man, can only be comprehended through the processes in which, and through which, he exists. The new dramatic art must methodologically incorporate the "experimental" in its form. It must be able to utilize associations in all directions; it needs static energy and has a tension which prevails in its individual parts and which "charges" these antithetically. (In other words, anything but a revue-like series of sketches.)

WHY MUST THE MOUNTED MESSENGER BE MOUNTED?

The Threepenny Opera presents a picture of bourgeois society (and not only of the "lumpen-proletariat" elements). This bourgeois society has, for its part, produced a bourgeois order of the world, and therefore has quite a distinct *Weltanschauung* without which it could probably not carry on. Whenever the bourgeoisie sees its own world represented, the appearance of the royal mounted messenger is absolutely inevitable. Mr. Peachum, when he is financially exploiting society's bad conscience, is trading on this very fact. Theatrical practitioners may care to ponder why nothing is more stupid than to abolish the *horse* of the mounted messenger — as nearly all modernistic producers of *The Threepenny Opera* have done. If one were representing a judicial murder on the stage, one could only pay proper tribute to the theatre's role in bourgeois society by having the journalist who discloses the innocence of the murdered man drawn into court by a swan. So cannot people realize how tactless it is to lure the public into laughing at itself by making the appearance of the mounted messenger a matter for mirth? Without the appearance of some form of mounted messenger, bourgeois literature would sink to a mere representation of circumstances. The mounted messenger guarantees really undisturbed enjoyment even of circumstances themselves unbearable, and is therefore a *conditio sine qua non* for a literature whose *conditio sine qua non* is lack of consequences.

Of course the third finale must be played with complete seriousness and extreme dignity.

— B. B.